Ivan Moscovich's
MASTERMIND COLLECTION

Perplexing Pattern Problems
& Other Puzzles

Sterling Publishing Co., Inc.
New York

To Anitta, Hila, and Emilia, with love

Ivan Moscovich Mastermind Collection:
Perplexing Pattern Problems & Other Puzzles was edited, designed, and typeset by
Imagine Puzzles Ltd., London (info@imaginepuzzles.com)

MANAGING EDITOR
David Popey
ART EDITOR
Keith Miller
CONSULTANT EDITOR
David Bodycombe
EDITORIAL ASSISTANT
Rosemary Browne
PUBLISHING DIRECTOR
Hal Robinson

Clipart: Nova Development Corporation

Library of Congress Cataloging-in-Publication Data Available

2 4 6 8 10 9 7 5 3 1

Published by Sterling Publishing Co., Inc.
387 Park Avenue South, New York, NY 10016
© 2005 by Ivan Moscovich
Distributed in Canada by Sterling Publishing
c/o Canadian Manda Group, 165 Dufferin Street,
Toronto, Ontario, Canada M6K 3H6
Distributed in Great Britain by Chrysalis Books Group PLC
The Chrysalis Building, Bramley Road, London W10 6SP, England
Distributed in Australia by Capricorn Link (Australia) Pty. Ltd.
P.O. Box 704, Windsor, NSW 2756, Australia

Sterling ISBN 1-4027-2345-8

For information about custom editions, special sales, premium and corporate purchases, please
contact Sterling Special Sales Department at 800-805-5489 or specialsales@sterlingpub.com

Contents

Introduction

Ever since my high school days I have loved puzzles and mathematical recreational problems. This love developed into a hobby when, by chance, some time in 1956, I encountered the first issue of *Scientific American* with Martin Gardner's mathematical games column. And for the past 50 years or so I have been designing and inventing teaching aids, puzzles, games, toys, and hands-on science museum exhibits.

Recreational mathematics is mathematics with the emphasis on fun, but, of course, this definition is far too general. The popular fun and pedagogic aspects of recreational mathematics overlap considerably, and there is no clear boundary between recreational and "serious" mathematics. You don't have to be a mathematician to enjoy mathematics. It is just another language, the language of creative thinking and problem-solving, which will enrich your life, like it did and still does mine.

Many people seem convinced that it is possible to get along quite nicely without any mathematical knowledge. This is not so: Mathematics is the basis of all knowledge and the bearer of all high culture. It is never too late to start enjoying and learning the basics of math, which will furnish our all-too sluggish brains with solid mental exercise and provide us with a variety of pleasures to which we may be entirely unaccustomed.

In collecting and creating puzzles, I favor those that are more than just fun, preferring instead puzzles that offer opportunities for intellectual satisfaction and learning experiences, as well as provoking curiosity and creative thinking. To stress these criteria, I call my puzzles Thinkthings.

The *Mastermind Collection* series systematically covers a wide range of mathematical ideas, through a great variety of puzzles, games, problems, and much more, from the best classical puzzles taken from the history of mathematics to many entirely original ideas.

This book includes a group of challenging puzzles based on problems involving the moves and positions of different chess figures, the most famous among them being the *Eight Queens Problem*. Other puzzles deal with the four color problem, balancing problems, Möbius strip, knots, and a diverse variety of other puzzles.

A great effort has been made to make all the puzzles understandable to everybody, though some of the solutions may be hard work. For this reason, the ideas are presented in a highly esthetic visual form, making it easier to perceive the underlying mathematics.

More than ever before, I hope that these books will convey my enthusiasm for and fascination with mathematics and share these with the reader. They combine fun and entertainment with intellectual challenges, through which a great number of ideas, basic concepts common to art, science, and everyday life, can be enjoyed and understood.

Some of the games included are designed so that they can easily be made and played. The structure of many is such that they will excite the mind, suggest new ideas and insights, and pave the way for new modes of thought and creative expression.

Despite the diversity of topics, there is an underlying continuity in the topics included. Each individual Thinkthing can stand alone (even if it is, in fact, related to many others), so you can dip in at will without the frustration of cross-referencing.

I hope you will enjoy the *Mastermind Collection* series and Thinkthings as much as I have enjoyed creating them for you.

—Ivan Moscovich

Is there an underlying structure to the beauty of the world? Do pattern and color have a mathematical reason for existing? Read on and you will be fascinated by the insights of modern math.

"The mathematician's patterns, like the painter's or the poet's, must be beautiful: the ideas, like the colors or words, must fit together in a harmonious way. Beauty is the first test: there is no permanent place in the world for ugly mathematics.
Godfrey Hardy (1877–1947)"

✳ Patterns in Mathematics

The world is made of colors and motion, feelings and thought.

Mathematics is the study of pure pattern; everything in the universe is a kind of pattern.

For the ancient Greeks, mathematics was the science of numbers. But this definition of mathematics has been incomplete for hundreds of years. In the middle of the 17th century, Isaac Newton in England and Gottfried von Leibniz in Germany independently invented calculus, the study of motion and change, and touched off an explosion in mathematical activity. Contemporary mathematics comprises 80 distinct disciplines, some of which are still being split into subcategories. So today, rather than focus on numbers, many mathematicians think their field is better defined as the science of patterns.

An interest with patterns is something that starts very early in our lives. And those patterns may take many forms—numerical, geometric, kinetic, behavioral, and so on. As the science of patterns, mathematics affects every aspect of our lives; abstract patterns are the basis of thinking, of communication, of computation, of society, and even of life itself. Patterns are everywhere and everyone sees them, but mathematicians see patterns within the patterns. Yet despite the somewhat imposing language used to describe their work, the goal of most mathematicians is to find the simplest explanations for the most complex patterns.

Part of the magic of mathematics is how a simple, amusing problem can lead to far-reaching insights.

Realizing the importance of this kind of thinking, many schools are mixing more geometry, topology, and probability into the math curriculum. This is all to the good: wherever there is relationship and pattern, there is mathematics.

▶ MONDRIAN GALLERY

In each set of four artworks at right, there is only one genuine Mondrian, plus three computer imitations.

Can you find the real Mondrians?

ANSWER: PAGE 98

Fascinating experiments like this were devised by Michael Noll of Bell Labs in the early '60s, in which he analysed Mondrian's creations and produced random computer graphics using the same elements.

He reported that 59% of the people who were shown both the Mondrian and the computer versions preferred the latter, 28% identified the computer pictures correctly, and 72% thought that the Mondrian was done by computer.

Such experiments provide food for thought. They may prove that a well-produced computer program can be as meaningful artistically as the intuition of the traditional artist.

❋ Pattern recognition

Pattern recognition is the research area that studies the operation and design of systems that recognize patterns in data. Patterns are recognized by perceiving significant similarities or differences in ideas, events, or physical phenomena. Detecting patterns is a way of creating order out of chaos, an attempt to give form to the world.

Structure is a set of relations between the entities of a pattern. Pattern concerns itself with relationships and symmetries, and is the simplest way of comprehending transformations. Structures are apt to be hierarchical. To achieve a hierarchy of structures and patterns, it is necessary to describe the patterns quantitatively. Two important quantitative systems of describing relations within and between patterns are topology and symmetry.

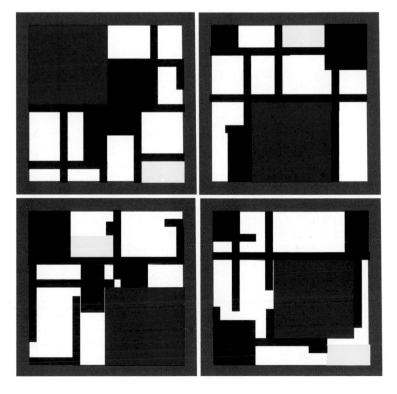

The most intricate patterns are often made from the most simple elements. Next time you look at a seemingly complicated arrangement count the shapes used. You'll be surprised.

> "A mathematician, like a painter or a poet, is a maker of patterns. If his patterns are more permanent than theirs, it is because they are made with ideas."
> *Godfrey Hardy, mathematician*

▲ MINIMAL ART

Mr. Matrisse is an artist, a minimalist. In spite of this, he is highly acclaimed for the visual diversity of his creations.

Can you figure out how many different basic elements were used in his latest exhibition of six giant panels?

ANSWER: PAGE 98

" olutions to problems are easy to find:
The problem's a great contribution
What's truly an art is to wring from your mind
A problem to fit a solution.
Piet Hein (1905–1996) **"**

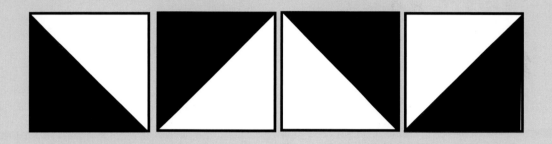

▲ MINIMAL STRIPS

Our pattern element is a single square divided by one of its diagonals into a two-color square, which can be rotated into four different orientations as shown above.

How many different colored linear patterns can you create by joining three element squares in a row?

ANSWER: PAGE 98

What can at first appear to be an easy problem can often turn out to be quite complex. Look carefully at the problems posed on these pages.

"**F**acts compel me to conclude that my brain was never formed for much thinking."
Charles Darwin (1809–1882)

▲ PERCEPT

How long will it take you to find the four five-color sequences shown in the middle of the pattern along the outer radial color lines?

ANSWER: PAGE 98

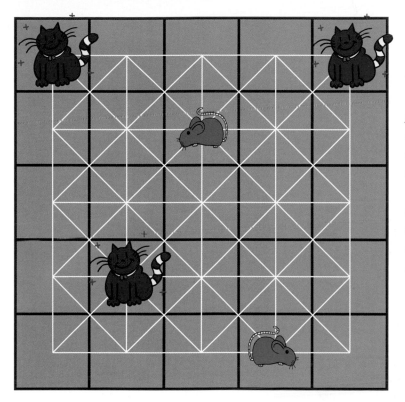

◀ LOOKING AT CATS AND MICE

Three cats and two mice are placed in the gameboard so that the cats can't see the mice and the mice can't see the cats. (The cats and mice can only see along the straight horizontal, vertical, and diagonal lines.)

Is it possible to place one more cat and two more mice under the same conditions? You are not permitted to change the locations of the cats and mice already on the gameboard.

ANSWER: PAGE 99

▶ MORE CATS AND MICE

Can you place four cats and four mice on the gameboard, so that (according to the rules of the previous puzzle) the cats can't see the mice and the mice can't see the cats?

Only one cat or mouse is allowed to occupy any one cell on the gameboard.

ANSWER: PAGE 99

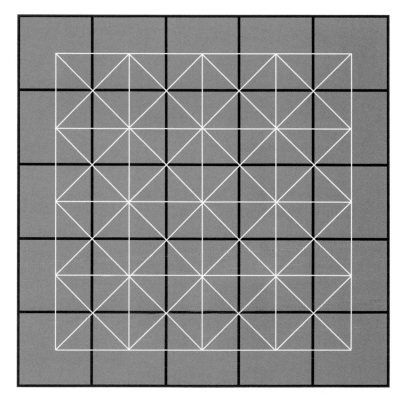

It's often thought that the division of anything implies the destruction of the whole, but this is not always the case. Different parts can work together, proving that the sum of the parts really is greater than the whole.

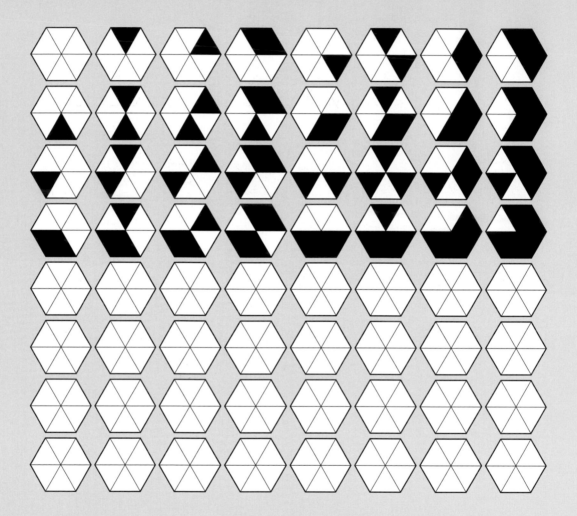

▲ HEXABITS 1—I CHING

Using two colors to color the edges of a regular hexagon, you can create exactly 64 different hexagons.

Half of the colored hexagons are shown.

Can you color the rest? (Rotations are considered to be different.)

Once you have the complete set of 64 hexagons you can play a game covering the hexagon gameboard (opposite) with the tiles so that adjacent sides of the tiles always match colors. (Three tiles will be left over.)

The structure of our hexabits puzzle is analogous to the I Ching or "Book of Changes" or "Oracle of Change," the oldest book on permutations and divination, still studied all over the world. It dates back to the 8th century B.C.

ANSWER: PAGE 99

▲ HEXABITS 2—YIN AND YANG

Use any 61 pieces from the previous page to fill this grid, so that adjacent pieces share an edge of the same color in the standard dominoes fashion.

ANSWER: PAGE 99

Photographic negatives are fascinating; light becomes dark and vice versa in a bizarre reversal of our everyday expectations. It's literally a whole new way of seeing the world.

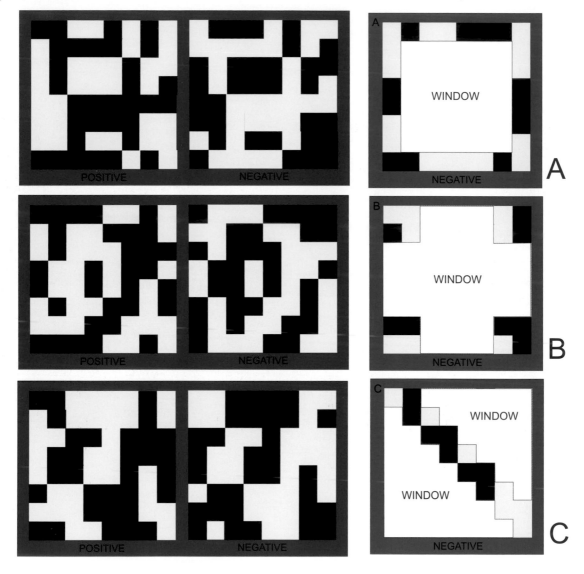

▲ EXACT NEGATIVES

Each image of these three pairs should be an exact inverse of the other. Black areas on one should be yellow on the other and vice versa.

One of the three masks A, B, and C, if placed over the right-hand image of each pair, will make all the pairs into exact inverses.

Which one?

ANSWER: PAGE 99

▲ POOL ACCIDENT

The heavy bowling ball near the pool may fall into the water or into the inflatable boat.

Which will raise the pool's water level by the greater amount:

1) The heavy ball falling into the boat, or

2) The heavy ball falling into the pool?

ANSWER: PAGE 100

The triangles and squares on these pages can form the basis for simple visual code systems. Think about how you might be able to manipulate the results to create your own cipher.

▶ **COLORING SQUARES**

A square is dissected into eight regions of equal area.

Coloring any two of these regions, we get a quarter-coloring of the square.

Coloring four of these regions, we get a half-coloring of the square.

Not counting reflections and/or rotations as different, in how many different ways can you quarter-color and half-color the square?

PUZZLE 1 *Can you find the 6 different quarter-colorings?*

PUZZLE 2 *Can you find the 13 different half-colorings?*

ANSWER: PAGE 100

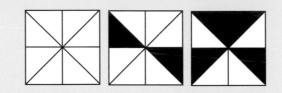

A square dissected into eight regions of equal area

Quarter-coloring

Half-coloring

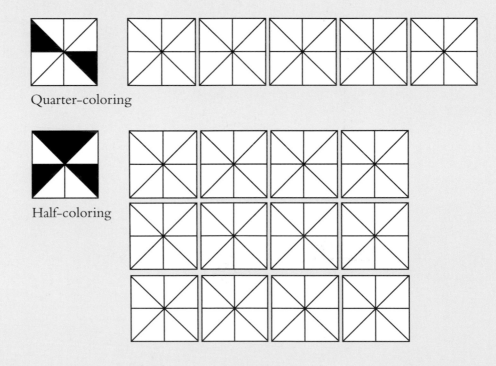

Quarter-coloring

Half-coloring

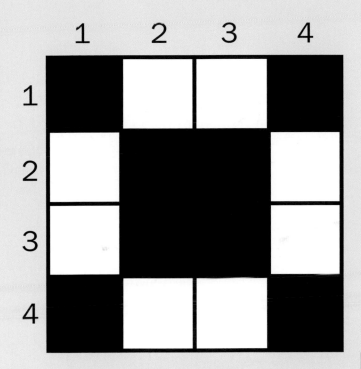

◄ BINARY PATTERNS

The squares of a 4-by-4 grid are colored black or white in the pattern shown at left.

The object is to transform all the squares of the grid into white squares, according to the following rules:

In a move you can choose any row or column and change the color of all the squares in that row or column from white to black and from black to white. You may repeat these moves any number of times.

What is the smallest number of moves to obtain the goal of having all white squares?

ANSWER: PAGE 100

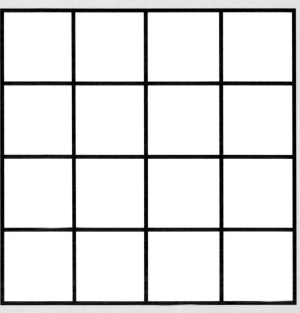

Jewelers are constantly trying to create the perfect necklaces for their customers. With all the possible combinations of stones they must understand a lot about the principles of pattern to make the best pieces.

▼ BEADS AND NECKLACES

You have a supply of beads in three colors—red, green, and yellow. The necklaces to be created consist of five beads each, and for each necklace two beads are to be of one color, two of a second color, and one of a third color.

How many distinct necklaces can be created?

ANSWER: PAGE 100

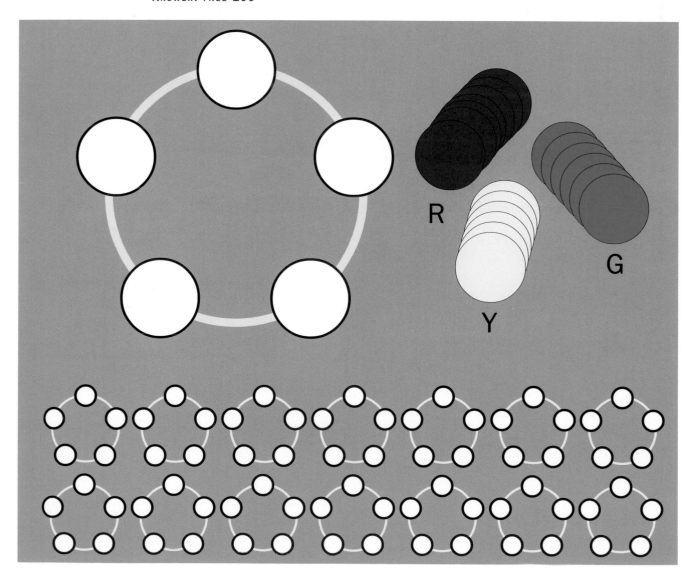

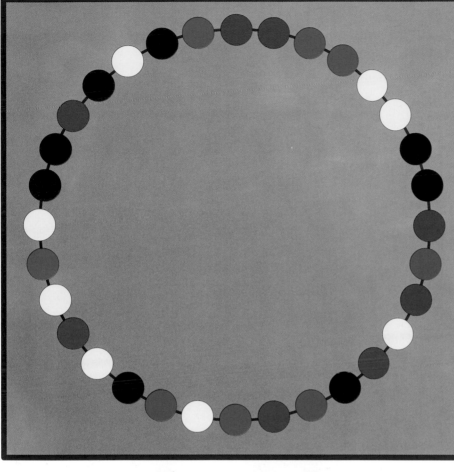

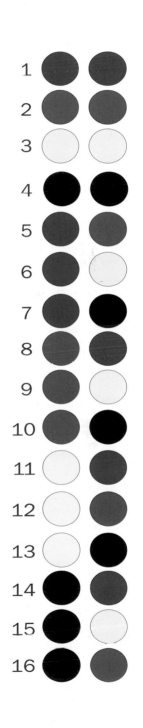

▲ PAIRING NECKLACE

Using a supply of beads of four colors, your objective is to create a closed necklace on which, if you go around it in either direction, each of the 16 possible color pairs would occur once.

This would suggest a solution consisting of 32 beads as shown above, but you can see that some pairs occur more than once. So the problem becomes, how many beads will it take to make the minimal necklace fulfilling the above objective?

ANSWER: PAGE 100

Sometimes you think you can see the answer to a problem straight away but often you're mistaken. Try the anagrams on these pages and test the power of your intuition.

▲ ANAGRAM 1

Rearrange the above letters to form a common word. There are two such words; can you find them?

ANSWER: PAGE 101

▲ ANAGRAM 2

Unscramble the above letters into a common six-letter noun.

ANSWER: PAGE 101

❋ Anagrams and artificial intelligence

An anagram is a word, phrase, or sentence formed by reordering the letters of another word, phrase, or sentence. Anagrams were used by the ancient Greeks as early as 260 B.C., and ever since have had a rich history of sacred symbolism. In the ancient world, they were thought to contain hidden messages from the gods. The mystical teachings of the Kabbala drew heavily on anagrams. The Romans also considered the study of anagrams as important. Anagrams are still very popular.

Computers have been able to accomplish great feats in large-scale computation. A computer named Grape can perform more than a trillion calculations every second as it computes the locations of individual stars within a cluster of stars. Another computer named Deep Blue was programmed to play out thousands of possible chess moves in advance so that it could defeat the human world champion.

Now computer scientists want to do something even more difficult: they want to program a computer to think the way humans do. The research has obtained some interesting results. Yet some of the abilities that add up to intelligence—abilities as simple as solving puzzles or predicting the next number in the sequence 1, 1, 2, 3, 5, 8, 13—have remained elusive. Generally people can do without thinking what computers cannot do at all.

The computer scientist Douglas Hofstadter has written a program designed to unscramble anagrams. In one way it's a trivial program. It would be easy to let a computer solve anagrams by mechanically listing every possible permutation of the letters and checking the results against a dictionary. Programs like that, which rely on raw, stupid computing power wouldn't even qualify as artificial intelligence. But Hofstadter wants a program to do its thinking in the same way a human does, deep below the level of consciousness, without logic. He wants a program that has an understanding of how words are put together. His anagram program is called Jumbo. It does not yet work as Hofstadter hopes it someday will. Perhaps this is because computers don't yet know how to be bored. They can't tell when they have fallen into a repetitious, machine-like rut. In solving problems that lack definite answers—doing anagrams without the help of a dictionary, for example—a machine needs to develop a sense of when it has gotten close enough to stop.

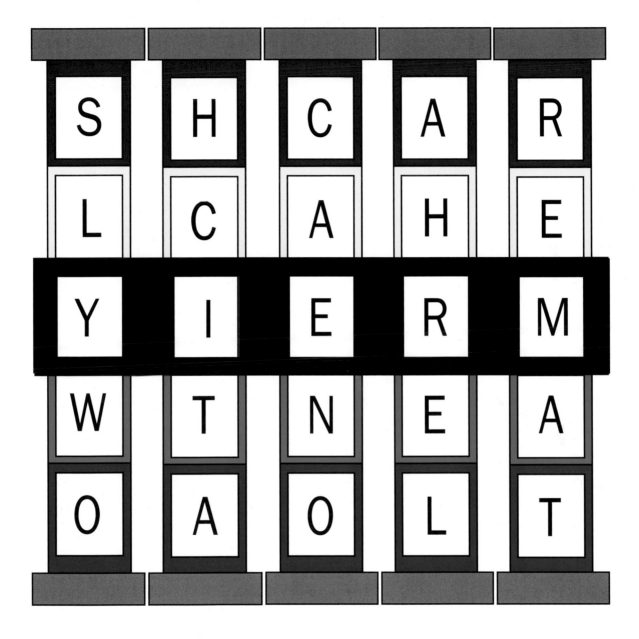

▲ WORD STRIPS

The five vertical strips can be pulled up and down in the fixed black frame to create five-letter words in the windows of the frame.

Can you find more than ten five-letter words? (Proper nouns are not allowed.)

ANSWER: PAGE **101**

When solving pattern puzzles, logic commands us to see connections between symbols and place them in an appropriate sequence. It's interesting to try to make yourself aware of how your mind does this.

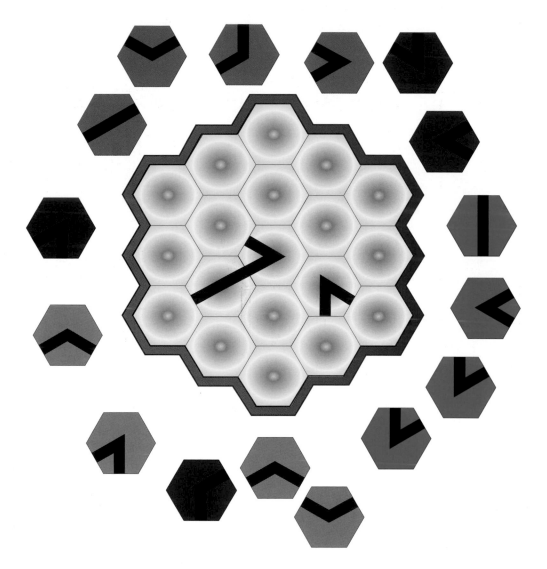

▲ HEXAGON LOOP

Fit in the 16 hexagons in the gameboard to complete a closed black line. The tiles cannot be rotated. For an extra challenge, see if you can find a solution that avoids placing a tile next to a hexagon of the same color.

ANSWER: PAGE 101

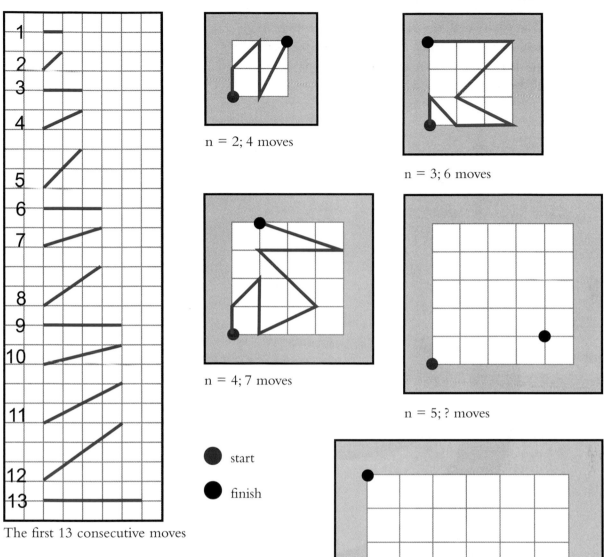

The first 13 consecutive moves

n = 2; 4 moves

n = 3; 6 moves

n = 4; 7 moves

● start
● finish

n = 5; ? moves

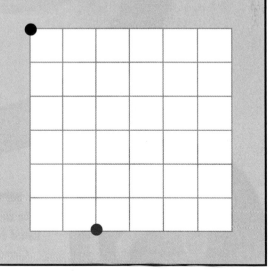

n = 6, ? moves

SQUARE ROUTES

Starting from a chosen point, consecutive lengths are added as shown in the examples above.

The object of the game is to draw as many consecutive lengths as possible and finish the line at a given end point. The line may not cross itself.

Solutions are given for n = 2, 3, and 4. Can you find the best solutions (the longest possible line) for n = 5 and n = 6? A more difficult version of this puzzle appears on page 90.

ANSWER: PAGE 102

If at first you don't succeed, try again. That's the maxim most people use to justify using perspiration instead of inspiration when trying to solve a problem. Let's hope these pages don't get you into a sweat.

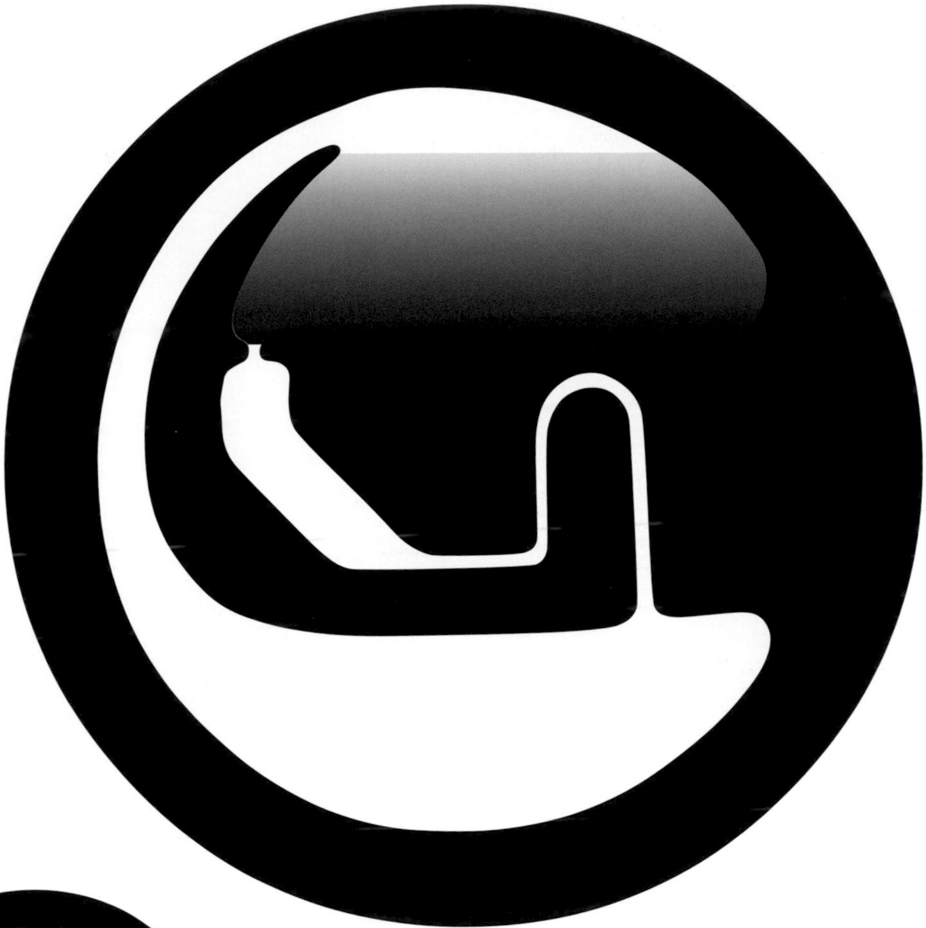

▲ SIPHON SYSTEMS

In the hermetically sealed model shown at left, liquid is stored in the lower compartment.

Can you describe what will happen when the model is quickly turned over?

ANSWER: PAGE 102

E	O			S	H
S	I	H	T	K	
R	E	W	T	O	R
	T	A	R	B	S
F	D		N	O	E
U		I	R	U	T

▲ COLOR CRYPTOGRAM

Can you decipher the secret message?

ANSWER: PAGE 102

"Don't wait for inspiration.
Work inspires inspiration.
If you succeed, keep working.
If you fail, keep working.
If you are interested, keep working.
If you are bored, keep working.
It works."
Michael Crichton

I t takes a certain and precise combination of occur-
rences to make most things happen, be they world
events or simple everyday tasks. Use this idea to investigate the puzzles below.

▲ CHAIN BALANCE

*One tray of a balance is filled with a chain, the other end of which is
firmly connected to the top of the tray on the other side of the balance.*

   *What will happen when we tilt and lower the side of the balance with
the empty tray as shown?*

ANSWER: PAGE 102

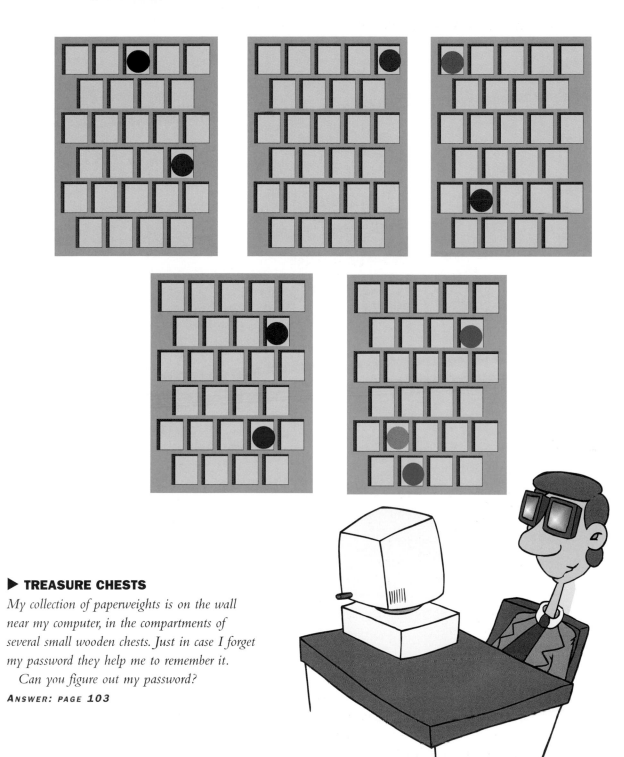

▶ TREASURE CHESTS

My collection of paperweights is on the wall near my computer, in the compartments of several small wooden chests. Just in case I forget my password they help me to remember it.

Can you figure out my password?

ANSWER: PAGE *103*

It's not only in science fiction stories that objects undergo unexpected transformations into different shapes. Topological transformations can teach us a lot about the similarity of seemingly different objects.

▲ TOPOLOGICAL TRANSFORMATION

Are the two interlocking structures above topologically equivalent?

In other words, if ou imagine the two structures are made of extremely elastic rubber material, can one be transformed into the other without breaking any of the loops? It may seem impossible but such a transformation can be done.

Can you work out how to do it?

ANSWER: PAGE 103

✳ Topology

Although we usually think of a flat surface as being literally "flat," in reality this may not be so. A surface has depth; it also has shape. In mathematics, understanding the properties of surfaces is called topology—which literally means the "logic of place," because it was first used to describe the landscape in geography. Folding is an extreme case of surfaces changing shape.

Topology is the study of continuity. It has become a cornerstone of modern mathematics. Topology is concerned with those properties of a figure that remain unchanged under continuous deformation; these are called topological invariants. The hole in a doughnut is a topological invariant. Continuous deformation is when the shape is bent, twisted, stretched, or compressed. Topology is often called rubber-sheet geometry. While other geometries study rigid shapes, angles, length, and curvature, topology deals with total flexibility. Topology, therefore, is the study of the properties of figures left invariant by topological transformations.

Examples of properties that are not topological include the angles of a triangle; by deforming a triangle it is possible to make the angles change. Similarly, the lengths of the sides of a triangle are not topological properties. Indeed, being a triangle is not a topological property: by introducing a bend in one side of a triangle, it can be continuously deformed into a quadrilateral, etc. In fact, to topologists, a triangle is the same as a square, a parallelogram—even a circle.

Clearly, little traditional geometry survives from the topological viewpoint.

So what properties are topological; what properties remain unchanged?

The fact that a triangle has an inside and an outside, and that it is impossible to pass from inside to the outside without crossing an edge of the triangle, is a topological property. No matter how a triangle is deformed in the plane, it will still possess an inside and an outside. In contrast, the fact that a bicycle wheel inner tube has a hole in the middle is a topological property; even a very distorted tube retains its hole. Many topological properties have to do with the way objects are or are not connected up. Whether or not a loop or a string is knotted is a topological property.

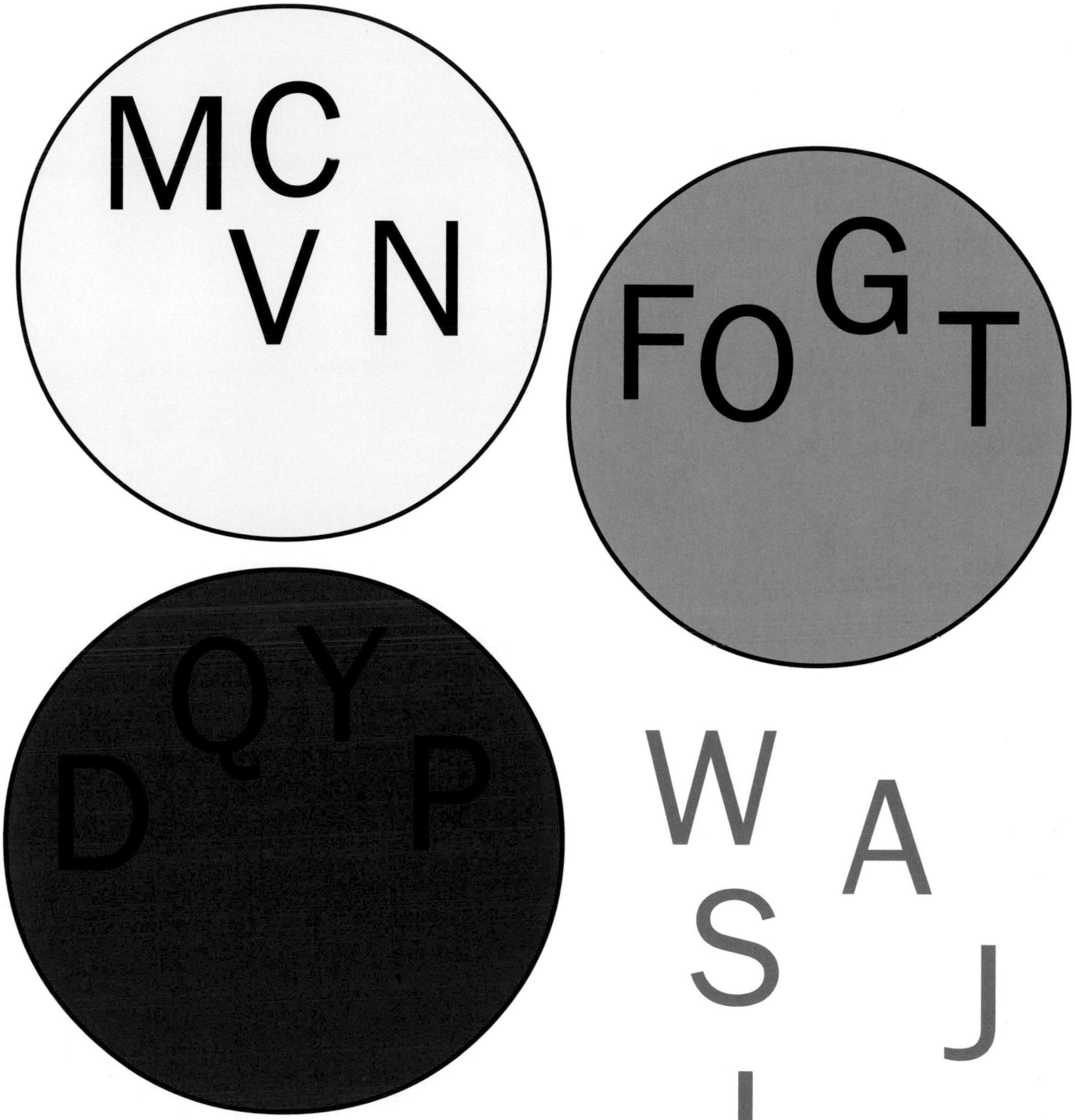

MC
VN

FO G T

QY
D P

W
A
S
J
U L R

▲ ALPHABET LOGIC

Place each blue capital letter into one of the three groups in the circles, matching them to a group in which they belong according to a topological rule. (The rules are left for you to figure out.)

Furthermore, find one letter in each circle that does not belong.

ANSWER: PAGE 103

Recognizing specific combinations of patterns is crucial in everyday life. How else would we obey traffic signals or color-coordinate our wardrobe to avoid unsightly clashes?

▼ PINWHEEL FOLDS

Copy and cut the puzzle along its outlines and along the blue lines.

Can you fold the ten flaps into the five-by-five square to form the pinwheel pattern shown at left? (You will actually be folding to the back of the paper, so you might want to copy the grid onto the back.)

ANSWER: PAGE 104

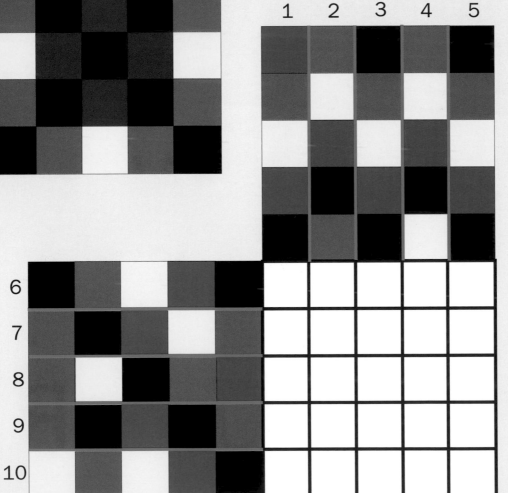

◀ FIFTH COLOR

In the April 1975 edition of Scientific American, mathematical correspondent Martin Gardner reported that William McGregor, a graph theorist of Wappingers Falls, New York, had constructed a map that could not be colored with fewer than five colors.

Below is an example of the completed map using five colors. Can you do any better?

ANSWER: PAGE 104

The fifth color

When maps were first colored it was often to denote separate territories or empires. Color coordination was a secondary thought; the main aim was to separate what was "mine" from what was "yours."

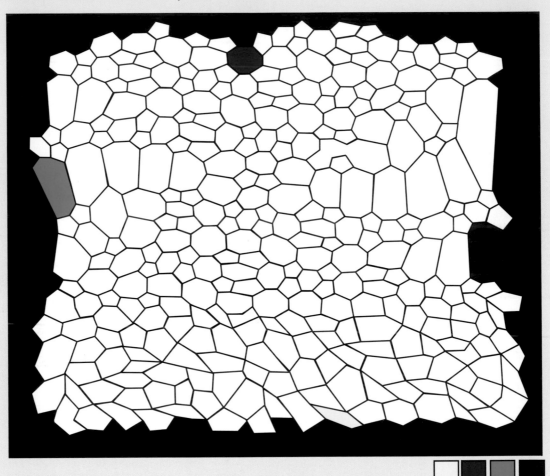

1 2 3 4

▲ FOUR-COLOR CROSSING

Color the pattern so that no two regions with a common border have the same color.

ANSWER: PAGE 105

TWO-PLAYER GAME

Try coloring the pattern according to the above rules. The first player who connects any two opposite sides with a continuous line of successive colors (1-2-3-4) is the winner.

❋ Four-color theorem

The four-color problem, stated in 1852 by Francis Guthrie, asked:

"How many colors are needed so that any map can be colored in such a way that no adjacent regions (which must touch along an edge, not just at a point) have the same color?"

The problem was unsolved until the late 1970s, when two mathematicians at the University of Illinois, Wolfgang Haken and Kenneth Appel, solved the problem using a supercomputer; we now have the four-color theorem, on which many puzzles and games are based.

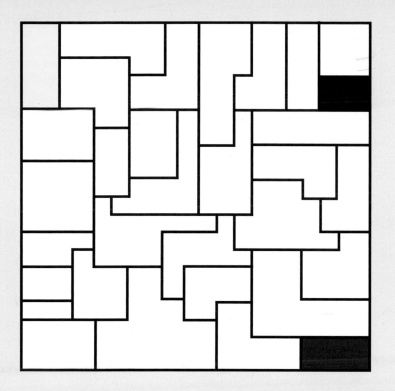

▶ COLORING PATTERNS

How many colors are needed for coloring the two patterns so that no two regions with a common border will have the same color?

Regions touching at a point can be colored in the same colors.

ANSWER: PAGE 105

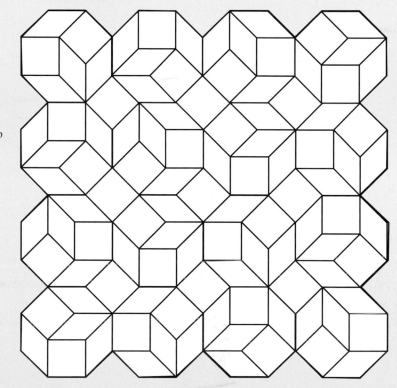

Maps communicate the idea of three-dimensional space in a simple yet effective way. When you look at them objectively, it's easy to marvel that we interpret them at all, let alone find our way around with them!

"Opportunity is missed by most people because it is dressed in overalls and looks like work.**"**
Thomas Edison

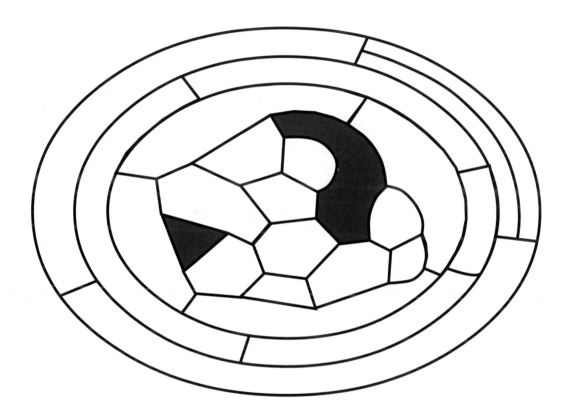

▲ M-PIRE PROBLEM

The famous "four-color problem" was solved by computer in the 1970s.

Herbert Taylor, from the University of Southern California, noted that the generalization of the problem of coloring maps is to consider a map in which each country or area to be colored consists of 'm' disconnected regions. With the requirement that all regions of a country must be colored in the same color, what is the smallest number of colors necessary for coloring such maps so that no two regions of the same color touch along a common border?

Under this generalization the four-color problem is a special case where m = 1, and the number of colors is 4.

It is interesting to note that when m = 2 (each country has a colony of the same color) the solution to the problem was already proved in 1890 by Percy Heawood (1861–1955). He first proved that an "m-pire" map needs no more than 6m colors. He also produced an m = 2 map requiring 12 colors.

Above is Heawood's 2-pire map.

Can you color it using 12 colors? One 2-pire is sample colored.

ANSWER: PAGE 106

▼ SNARKS

How many colors will you need to color each line between two gray end points in the four graphs, so that no two lines of the same color meet at any end point? Lines are only considered to meet at the points marked.

ANSWER: PAGE **106**

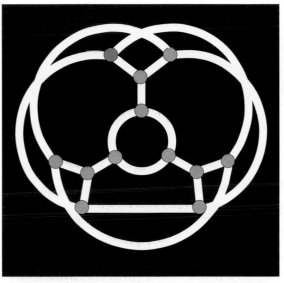

1

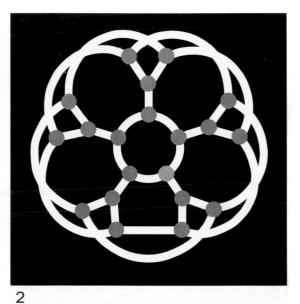

2

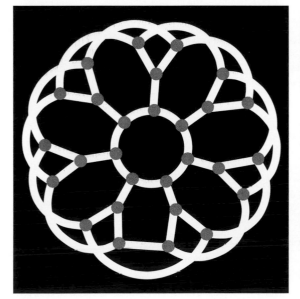

3

4

Sometimes, quite literally, how you look at a problem can change everything. On these pages, notice how the shape of a two-dimensional geometric form can affect our perception.

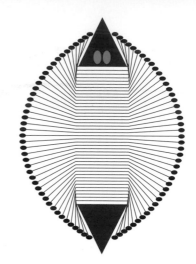

◀ **CENTER POINT**

Which of the six red points is the center of the big circle?

ANSWER: PAGE 106

▲ **MY CENTIPEDE**

Are all the horizontal lines of the "insect" of equal lengths?

ANSWER: PAGE 106

✳ Optical illusions

Among the most interesting of perceptual phenomena are optical illusions or, as they are sometimes called, "geometrical paradoxes."

In optical illusions we see things as we think they should be rather than as they are, because of our previous experiences and influences. This visual property of our perceptual system is widely applied in our daily lives, in science, math, art, and design. It should give us a warning as to the reliability of our observations and our senses in general, stressing the importance of measurement.

Optical illusions represent the other way that shapes can seem to change—the way we can see them change. The way we see things—or more precisely, the way we understand what we see—is also based on a set of rules. These are not written rules, but are learned by experience. Just as logical rules can seem to be broken in paradoxes, so the rules of perception can also seem to be wrong. When this happens, an illusion occurs. Understanding what can happen when this occurs helps us understand exactly how important the rules are in the first place, and how much we depend on them.

We can be made to believe things are larger than they are; we can be made to see depth in a two-dimensional flat surface, see colors where they aren't, see motion where there isn't any at all.

Much of perception is like a language that has to be learned. Our contact with the world is 90% through the eyes—all day long, until we close that apparatus to the world.

The visual system is not simply a camera, a direct receiver and recorder of information. Together, the eye and the brain are an organizing apparatus that analyzes and processes the large mass of data coming from the outside world. The visual apparatus is not only capable of eliminating the irrelevant and recognizing the unfamiliar, but as we shall see, it is also able to operate with limited information. It "fills in" where there are gaps. This may be called "the etcetera principle," meaning that when we see a few members of a series and an indication of the rest, it assumes the existence of them all.

Much of art is based on this tendency to fill in, to complete, to organize, and so is much of ordinary vision.

There is much more about perception in general that you can discover by pursuing the subject further. In any case, we should be aware that there is a limit to our senses and no amount of practice can ever make them good enough for some special tasks. The solution is to find ways to extend our senses—to invent tools capable of this. Fortunately, throughout history, humankind has always been successful in creating such tools whenever the need arose for them.

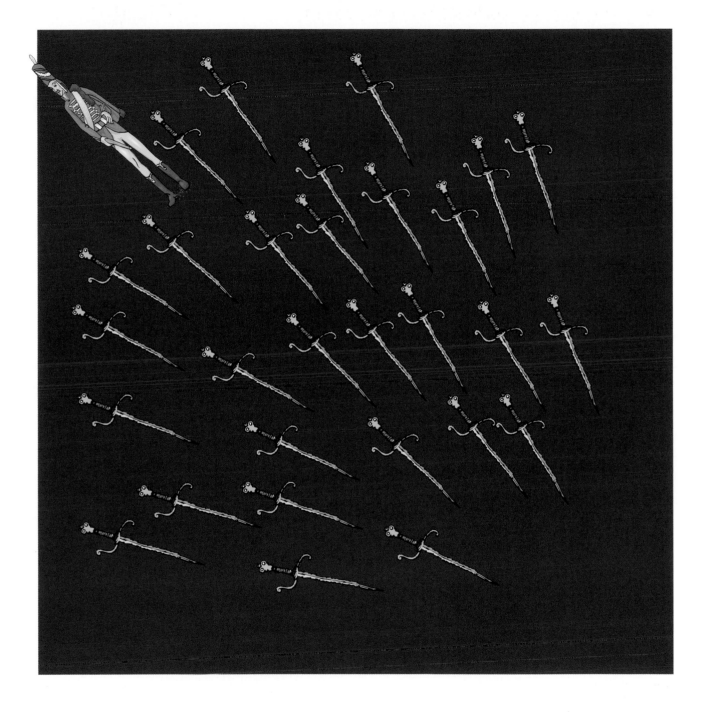

▲ VERTICAL SWORDS

How can you look at the swords to see them in three dimensions, sticking out vertically from the page?

ANSWER: PAGE 106

Even our own eyes cannot take in all the information on offer from the world, so it's no wonder simple drawings can sometimes baffle us. Our brains fill in gaps in our sight (for example, when we blink) and can be very deceptive.

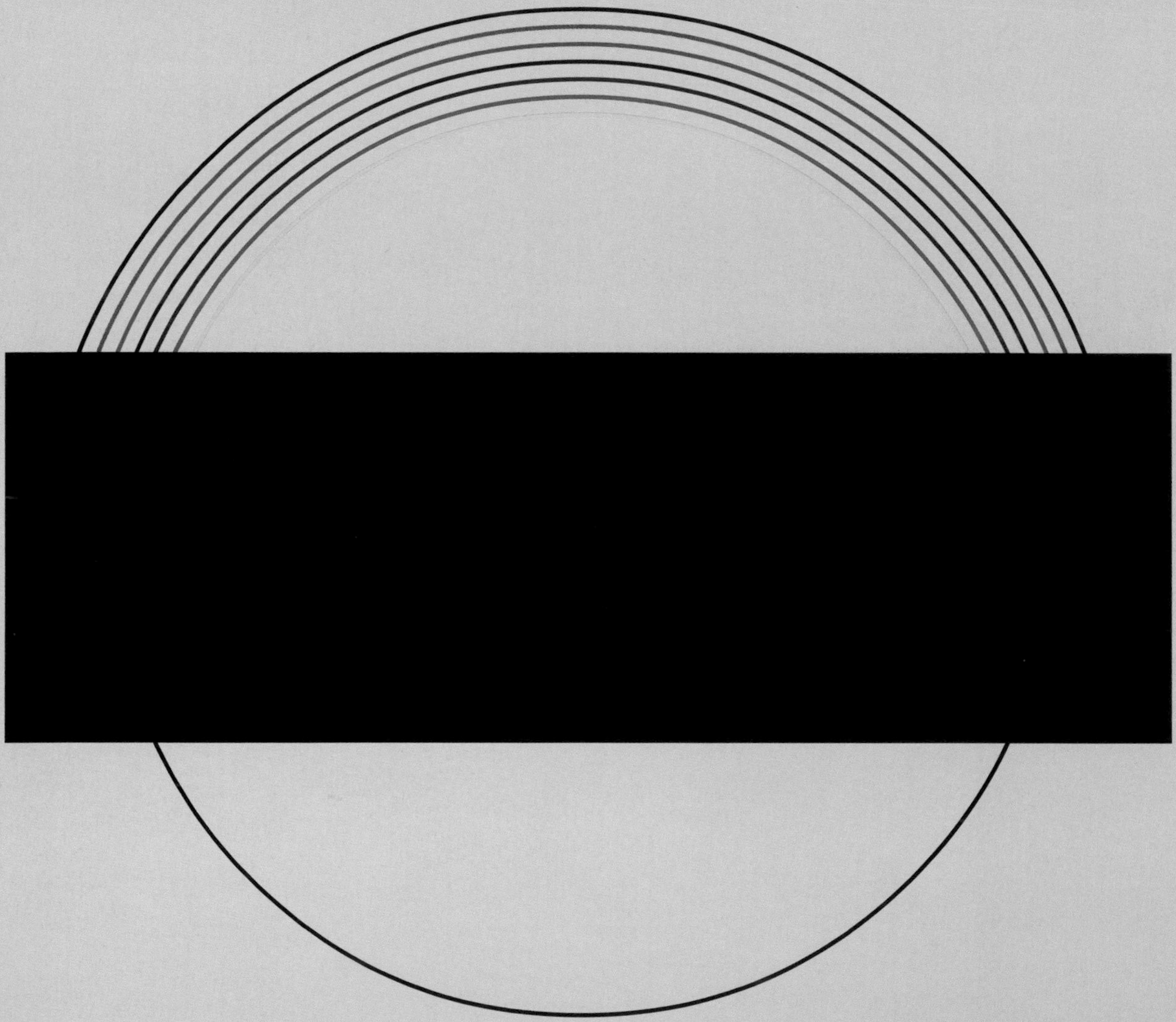

▲ INTERRUPTED CIRCLES

Just by looking, can you tell which of the colored lines is the continuation of the black circle passing behind the black block?

ANSWER: PAGE 106

▼ INTERRUPTED LINES

Without using a straightedge, can you tell which of the colored lines are the continuations of the two black lines passing behind the black block?

ANSWER: PAGE 107

Inside and outside are among the most obvious of opposites, but what if the distinctions were blurred, as in the Möbius strip?

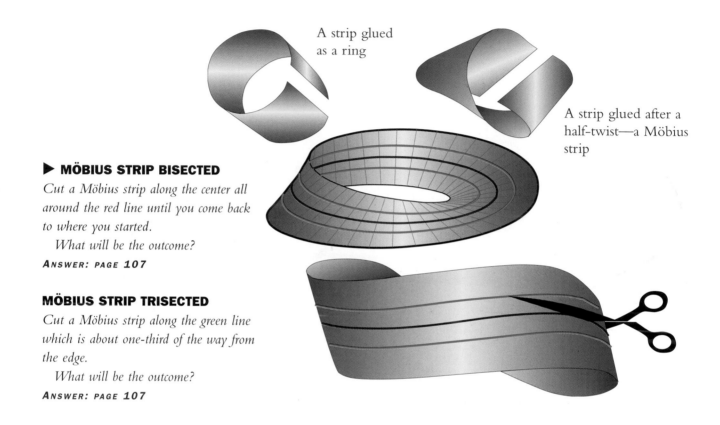

A strip glued as a ring

A strip glued after a half-twist—a Möbius strip

▶ MÖBIUS STRIP BISECTED

Cut a Möbius strip along the center all around the red line until you come back to where you started.

What will be the outcome?

ANSWER: PAGE 107

MÖBIUS STRIP TRISECTED

Cut a Möbius strip along the green line which is about one-third of the way from the edge.

What will be the outcome?

ANSWER: PAGE 107

A.F. Möbius (1790–1868)

The 19th-century German mathematician A.F. Möbius discovered that it was possible to make a surface that has only one side and one edge and has no "inside" and "outside." Although such an object seems impossible to imagine, making a Möbius strip is very simple: take a strip of ordinary paper and give one end a twist, then glue the two ends together. A Möbius strip is the basis of an endless number of exciting structures and puzzles with many surprising and paradoxical properties that have led to meaningful developments in topology.

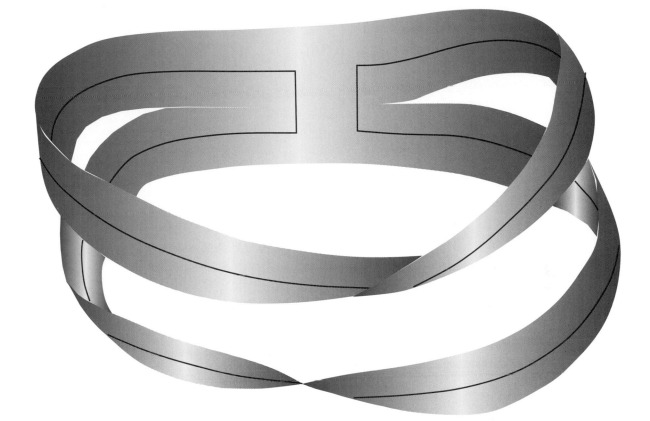

A			B
B			A
A'			B'
B'			A'

▲ SIAMESE MÖBIUS STRIP

Take a strip of paper and cut two longitudinal slots as shown. Bring the upper pair of ends together and join with a half-twist so that A joins A, and B joins B.

Then do the same with the lower pair of ends, but twisting in the opposite direction, joining A' to A', and B' to B'.

The result will look like the structure above.

Can you visualize what the outcome will be if you cut the structure along the red lines?

ANSWER: PAGE 107

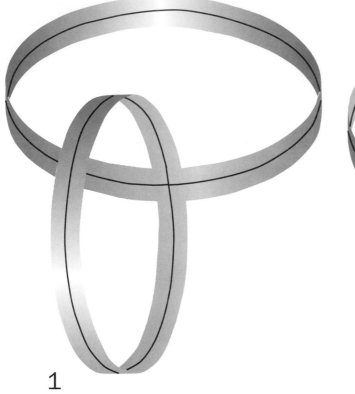

1

2

▶ MÖBIUS PAIRS

Each of the three paper structures shown here consists of two loops, one horizontal, the other vertical, and glued together at right angles at one point:

1) Two rings joined together
2) A ring and a Möbius strip
3) Two Möbius strips

Can you tell what the outcome will be if we cut the three structures along the red lines?

ANSWER: PAGE 107

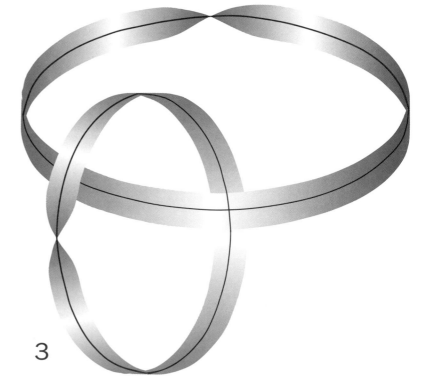

3

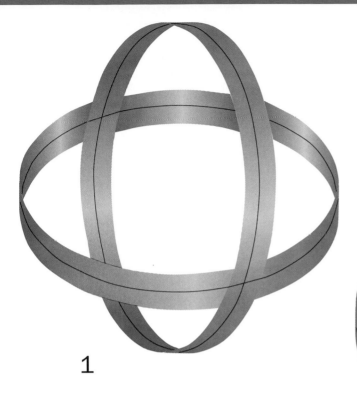

1

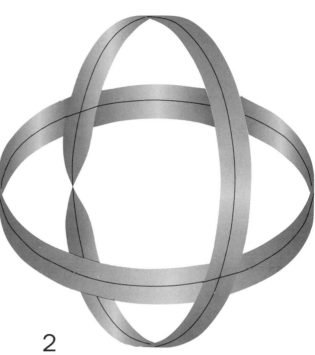

2

▶ MÖBIUS NESTED PAIRS

Each of the three paper structures shown here consists of two nested loops, one horizontal, the other vertical, glued together at right angles at two points:

    1) Two rings joined together

    2) A ring and a Möbius strip

    3) Two Möbius strips

    Can you tell what the outcome will be if we cut the three structures along the red lines?

ANSWER: PAGE 107

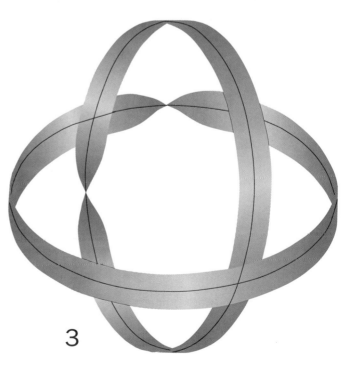

3

▲ SLOTTED RING

*Take a long strip of paper and cut two notches into each end. Both ends
of the strip should now have three different pieces.*

Glue together 1 and 4.

Pass 2 underneath 1, and 5 over 4, and glue 2 and 5 together.

Pass 6 over 5 and under 4, then glue 6 and 3 together.

*Now take some scissors and continue both cuts along the strip. What
will be the result?*

ANSWER: PAGE 107

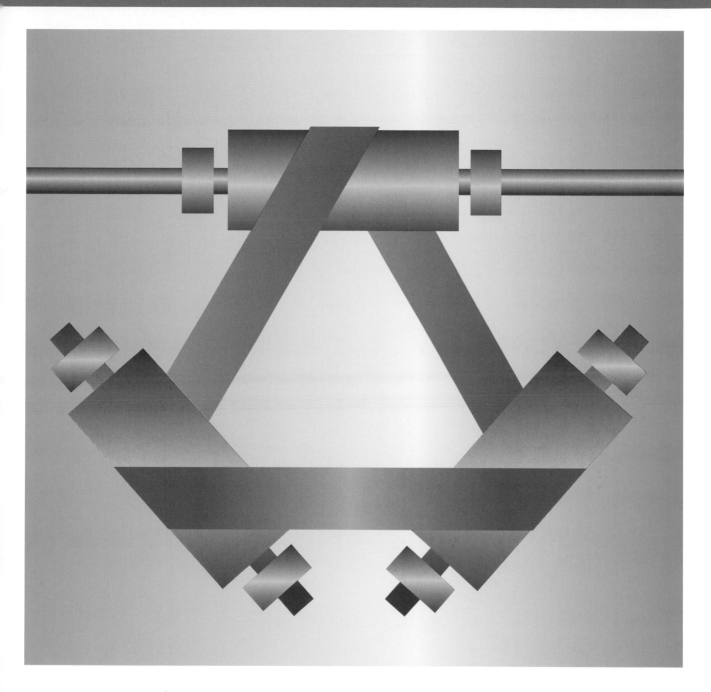

▲ BELT DRIVE

In the belt drive mechanism the belt is stretched between three cylindrical rollers driven by the top roller.

Can you tell what the form of the belt is and how it was constructed?

Take a long strip of paper and try to reconstruct the shape of the belt.
Is it just a simple ring, or a Möbius strip, or something else?

ANSWER: PAGE 108

Toplogy demands that we make sense of three-dimensional objects, whether they are inherently geometrical or conventionally more natural in appearance.

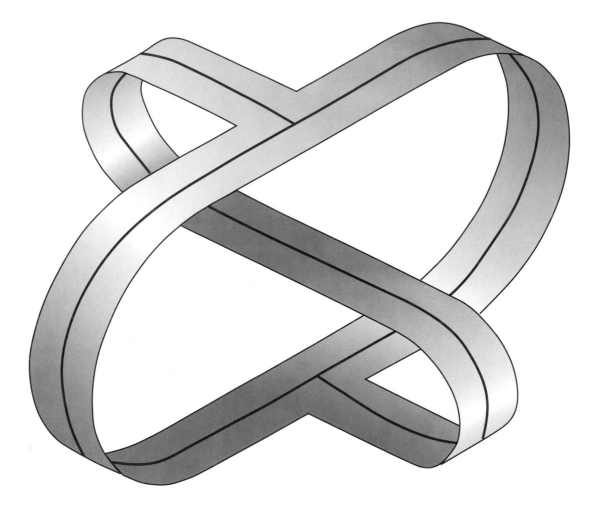

▲ MÖBIUS OR NOT?

Martin Gardner showed the above paper structure sent to him by Josiah Manning of Aurora, Missouri, asking his readers whether this surface is topologically equivalent to a Möbius strip.

Can you find the answer by working out what the outcome will be if we cut the surface along the red lines?

ANSWER: PAGE 108

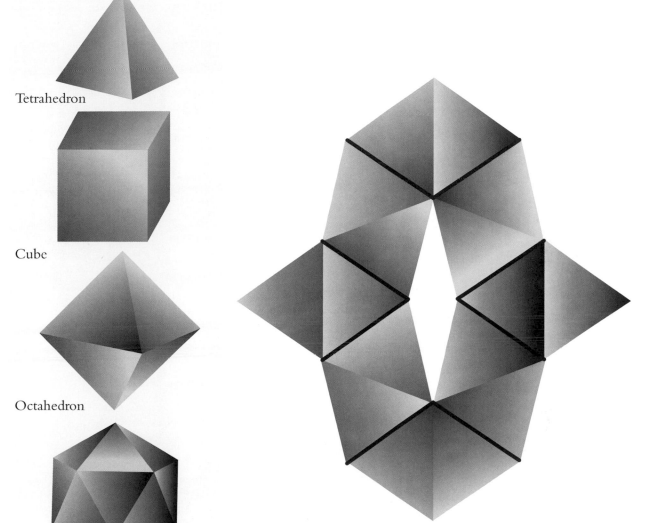

Tetrahedron

Cube

Octahedron

Icosahedron

Dodecahderon

▲ REGULAR POLYHEDRA RINGS

Joining eight regular octahedrons along their congruent faces can create a polyhedral ring with one hole, as shown above.

Can polyhedral rings be made in a similar manner from the rest of the regular polyhedra?

ANSWER: PAGE 108

▶ HOPSTIX

Hopstix is a race game between two players, each trying to transfer his or her playing pieces across the gameboard.

Each player has six playing pieces in three colors, one player with a set of circles, the other with squares.

Initially the pieces are placed on the starting rows at the two ends of the gameboard.

The Rules:

1) Players move their pieces one at a time into an adjacent empty space or jump over another piece to an empty space immediately beyond it.

2) Moves and jumps are allowed in all directions—forward, backward, sideways, and diagonally—but jumps must land on a space of the same color as the jumping piece.

3) As in standard checkers, multiple jumps in a move are allowed, but again the final landing must be on a square of the same color as the jumping piece (the intermediate jumps may be on squares of any color).

◄ **HOPSTIX**

Sample game.

It is the turn of the circles player. Who will win?

ANSWER: PAGE 108

Both children and adults learn more about a subject by playing games. The interconnected nature of the following challenges may reveal how much knowledge you already have inside you.

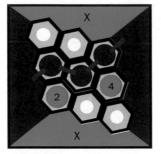

On a 2-by-2 board the player with the first move easily wins

On a 3–by–3 board the first player wins when his first move is the center cell

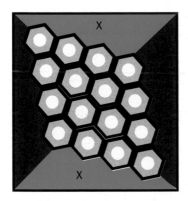

How and in how many moves can the first player win on a 4-by-4 gameboard?

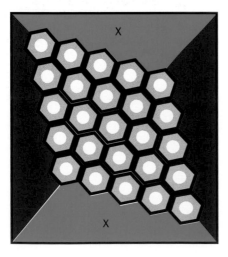

How can the first player win on a 5-by-5 gameboard?

◀ HEX GAME

One of the most interesting topological games is Hex, invented in 1942 by Piet Hein, a remarkable Danish inventor and freedom fighter. He invented Hex while analysing the four-color problem of topology. In 1948, John F. Nash, a Nobel prize winner at M.I.T., independently reinvented the game. The game was the first to introduce the concept of connectivity, the board-crossing principle on which many later games were based, like Twixt, Bridge-It, and others.

Although it is a very simple game to learn and play, it offers surprising mathematical subtleties.

Hex is played on an 11-by 11 hexagonal gameboard, but the size of the board can vary.

One player has a supply of red pieces; the other a supply of green. It can also be played as a paper-and-pencil game, using marks like "O" and "X."

Players alternate by placing their pieces on an unoccupied hexagonal cell (or mark the cell "O" or "X").

The object of the game is to complete an unbroken chain of a solid color from one side of the board to the other. The corner hexagons may belong to either of the two colors or marks.

No draw is possible; one player must win.

ANSWER: PAGE 108

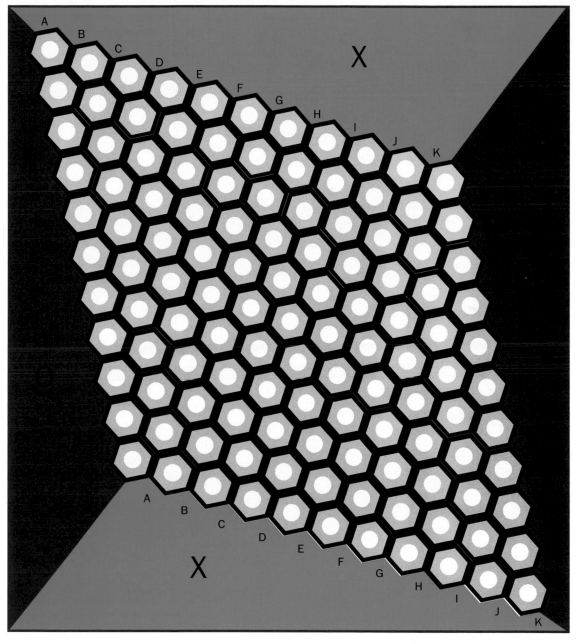

The standard gameboard for a two-person paper-and-pencil game.

You don't have to be an aficionado to know that tac-tical movement and strategic thinking is the name of the game when it comes to chess. Find out more on these pages.

❄ Knight's tours

The chess knight moves two squares horizontally and one vertically, or two vertically and one horizontally.

One of the oldest and most interesting chess puzzles is the knight's tour, which originated in 1700 with the English mathematician Brook Taylor: can the knight be made to visit every square of the board exactly once, by a series of legal moves? The size of the board need not be the usual 8-by-8 chessboard.

Mathematically, this is a question about graphs. Think of the squares on the board as nodes, and join the nodes by an edge if there is a legal knight's move that connects them. (That is, squares are not connected by adjacency in the ordinary sense, but in "knight's space.")

The tour is closed if the knight returns to his original home on the final move. Closed tours can only occur on even-sided boards. To see this, note that the knight changes the color of his square on each move, if the squares are in the usual checkered pattern. On an odd-sided board he makes an even number of moves to visit every square, so if he takes one more move to return to the square he started from, that move would have to be to a square colored differently than his starting square, which is clearly impossible.

On the standard chessboard there are several million different knight's tours. Euler found many with unusual symmetries.

You can create knight's tours by numbering the squares of the board to indicate the knight's progress. An alternative way of representing the same path is to draw a continuous line between the centers of the squares. The visual patterns created this way are often aesthetically pleasing. (Some original designs based on closed knight's tours are shown at right.) Copying the basic grid, you can color and preserve the tours.

It is also interesting to investigate knight's tours on rectangular and other boards.

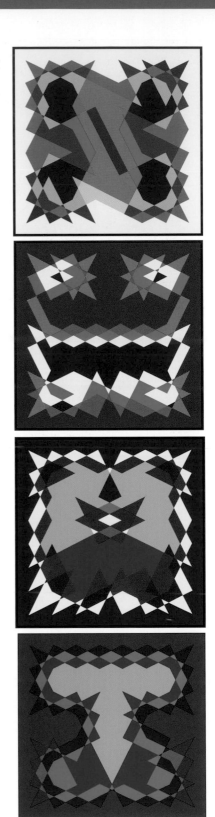

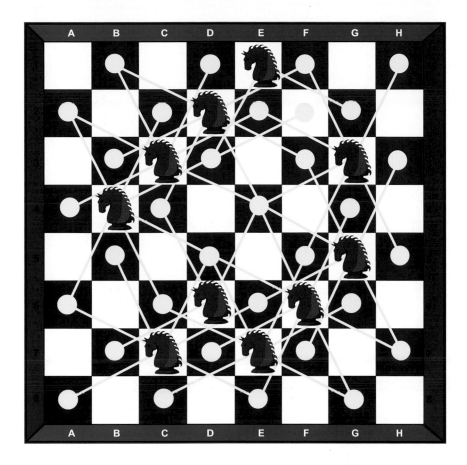

▲ KNIGHTS' BLACK ATTACK

We can see 10 knights placed so that all 32 black squares are attacked by at least one knight.

Can you find a better solution, using a smaller number of knights to achieve the same result? What is the minimum number of knights needed?

ANSWER: PAGE 109

▶ KNIGHTS' AVOIDANCE

What is the maximum number of knights you can place on a chessboard so that no knight is attacked by another?

ANSWER: PAGE 109

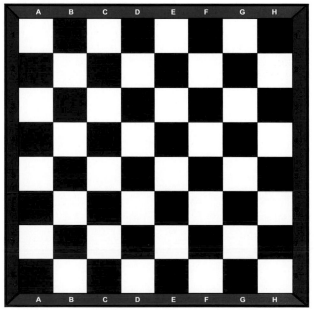

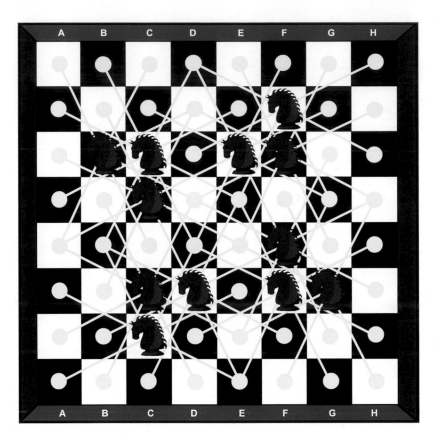

▶ KNIGHTS' ALL-OUT ATTACK 1

The 12 knights shown above are situated so that all 64 fields are either occupied or under attack.

You can observe that only four knights are under attack by another knight.

How many knights are needed to create a similar configuration in which all the knights are also under attack by another knight or knights?

ANSWER: PAGE 109

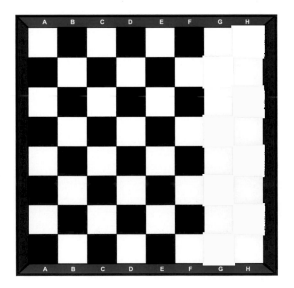

▶ KNIGHTS' ALL-OUT ATTACK 2 AND 3

What is the smallest number of knights you can place on a 9-by-9 and 10-by-10 board so that all unoccupied fields are under attack by at least one knight?

ANSWER: PAGE 109

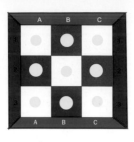

Puzzle 1
3-by-3 gameboard

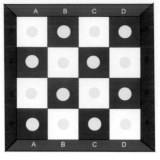

Puzzle 2
4-by-4 gameboard

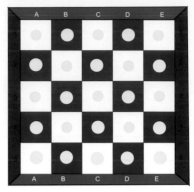

Puzzle 3
5-by-5 gameboard

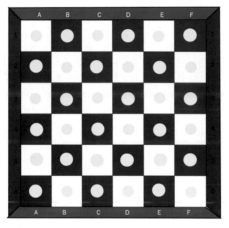

Puzzle 4
6-by-6 gameboard

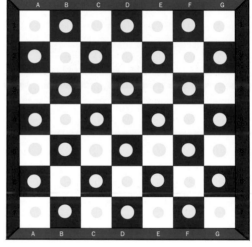

Puzzle 5
7-by-7 gameboard

▶ KNIGHT'S TOURS—UNCROSSED

*How far can a knight travel on each gameboard
without crossing its own path?*

ANSWER: PAGE 110

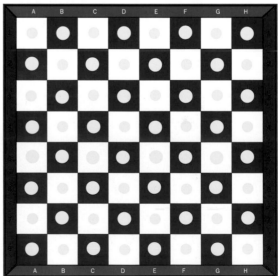

Puzzle 6
8-by-8 gameboard

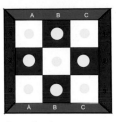

Puzzle 1
3-by-3
gameboard

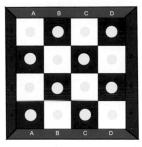

Puzzle 2
4-by-4 gameboard

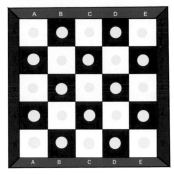

Puzzle 3
5-by-5 gameboard

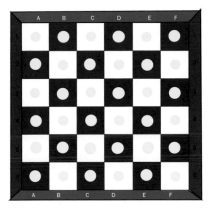

Puzzle 4
6-by-6 gameboard

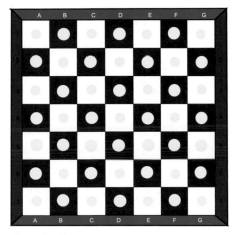

Puzzle 5
7-by-7 gameboard

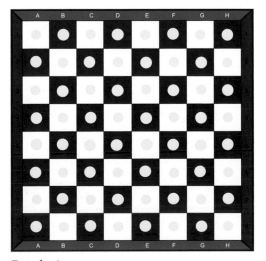

Puzzle 6
8-by-8 gameboard

▲ KNIGHT'S TOURS—CROSSED

Can you find complete knight's tours for the six chessboards? The knight's path may cross itself, unlike in the "uncrossed tours."

ANSWER: PAGE 111

If you've ever experimented with a magnifying glass to concentrate the sun's rays, you'll understand a little about how lenses work. But what happens when you're presented with a variety of different shapes and sizes?

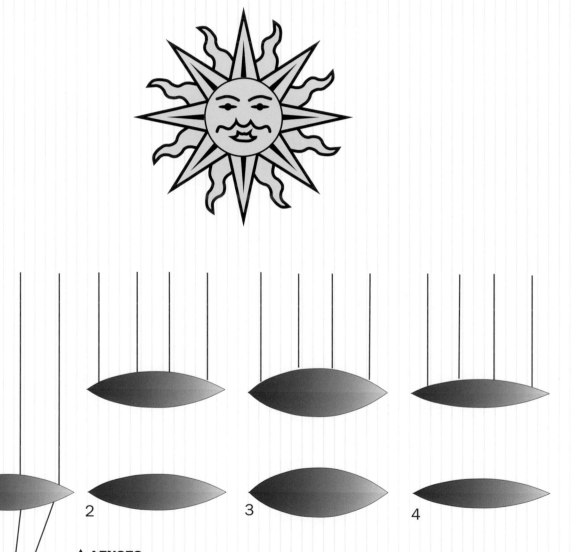

▲ LENSES

Convex or converging lenses are called positive lenses, because they cause parallel rays of light to converge to a point called the focus.

What will happen if two positive lenses of different thickness are placed next to each other?

Will the rays converge the same way as with one lens? If not, what will they do differently?

ANSWER: PAGE *112*

▲ BURNING LENSES

Sunlight is shining on a piece of paper through four lenses as shown.

Which of the lenses will set the sheet of paper on fire? If more than one lens will work, which will start the fire most efficiently?

ANSWER: PAGE 112

The phrase "a trick of the light" is used to explain a fleeting glimpse of an often unexplained phenomena. However there's nothing strange here—it's all explained by science.

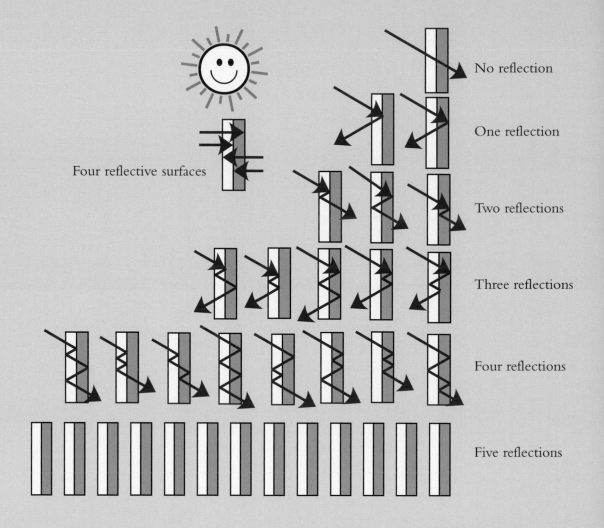

Four reflective surfaces

No reflection

One reflection

Two reflections

Three reflections

Four reflections

Five reflections

▲ LIGHT REFLECTION

Let us consider the phenomenon of light reflection. If two plates made from slightly different types of glass are mounted face to face, there are effectively four possible surfaces from which the light can bounce.

If the light does not reflect at all, there is only one way it can pass through the glass. If there is one reflection, there are two possible routes. For two reflections, there are three possibilities.

The pattern for the number of possible reflections becomes: 1, 2, 3, 5, 8, 13, 21.... This is known as the Fibonacci series, where each term is the sum of the two previous terms.

Can you draw the light rays for all 13 possible ways in which the light may be reflected five times?

ANSWER: PAGE 112

▲ GOLDFISH

When you look down into a goldfish bowl, do you see the fish as being the same size it would appear to be if there were no water in the bowl?

ANSWER: PAGE 112

Problems associated with various chess pieces and their placements have entertained puzzlists for centuries. The Eight Queens problem is a classic among such puzzles.

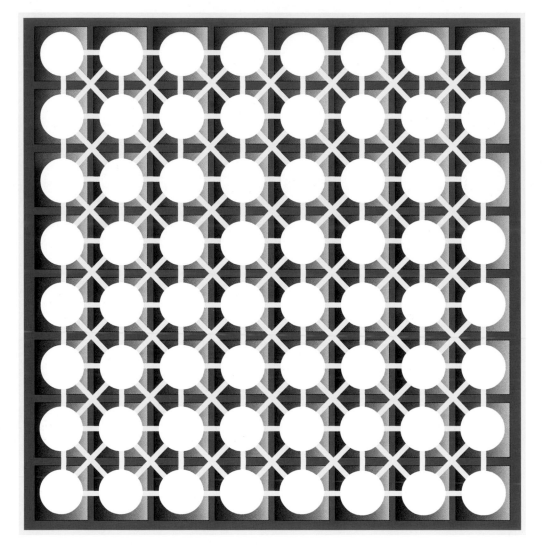

▲ THE EIGHT QUEENS PROBLEM

Can you place 8 chess queens on the chessboard so that no queen can be captured by another?

This problem was first posed in 1848 by Max Bezzel, and is considered a gem of recreational mathematics.

There are 12 basically different solutions.

How many can you find using the grids on the opposite page?

ANSWER: PAGE 113

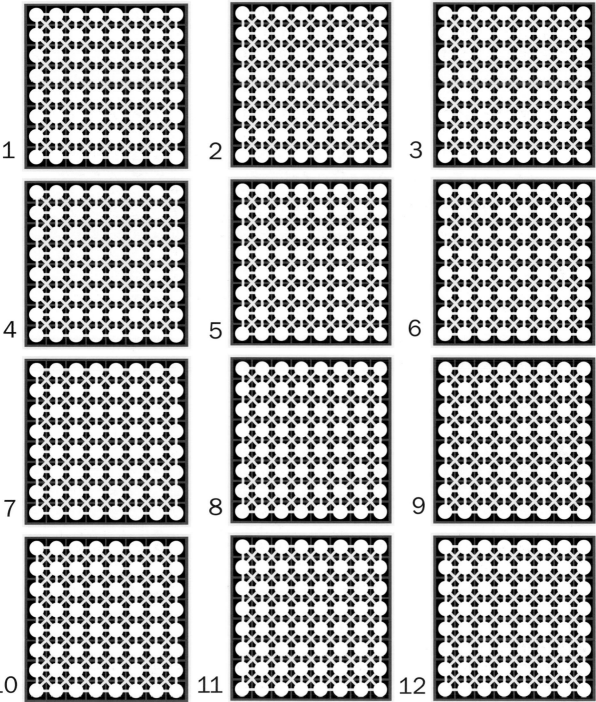

1

2

3

4

5

6

7

8

9

10

11

12

Puzzle 1

Puzzle 2

Puzzle 3

▶ QUEENS' MINI-STANDOFF

How many chess queens can you place on each board so that no queen can be captured by another?

ANSWER: PAGE 114

Puzzle 4

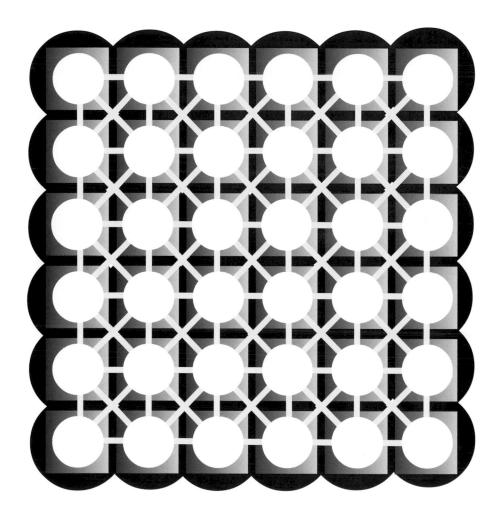

▲ QUEENS' COLOR STANDOFF 1

*Another interesting variation of the classical "Eight Queens Problem"
is the "Queens' Color Standoff Problem," involving the placement of sets
of differently colored queens:*

  *How many queens of two colors can be placed on boards of different
sizes so that no queen is attacked by a queen of the other color?*

  *Or, stated in a simpler form: no two or more differently colored queens
can be in any horizontal row, vertical column, or diagonal.*

  *Can you place 4 red queens and 6 blue queens on the board so that no
queen of one color is attacked by a queen of another color?*

ANSWER: PAGE 114

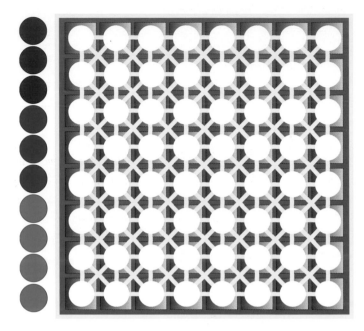

◄ QUEENS' COLOR STANDOFF 2

Can you place 3 red queens, 3 blue queens, and 4 green queens on a chessboard so that no queen of one color is attacked by a queen of another color?

ANSWER: PAGE **115**

► QUEENS' COLOR STANDOFF 3

Can you place 9 red queens and 10 blue queens on a chessboard so that no queen of one color is attacked by a queen of another color?

ANSWER: PAGE **115**

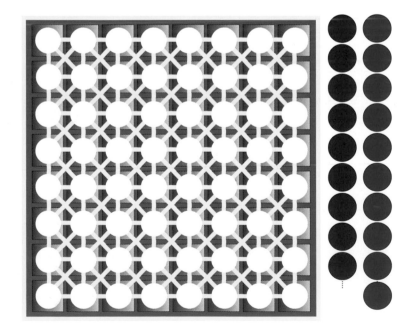

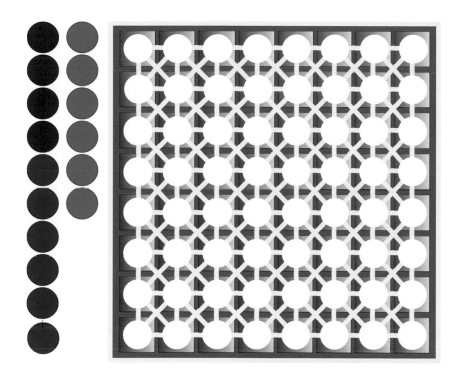

◄ QUEENS' COLOR STANDOFF 4

Can you place 4 red queens, 5 blue queens, and 6 green queens on a chessboard so that no queen of one color is attacked by a queen of another color?

ANSWER: PAGE 115

► QUEENS' COLOR STANDOFF 5

Can you place 3 red queens, 3 blue queens, 3 green queens, and 3 yellow queens on a chessboard so that no queen of one color is attacked by a queen of another color?

ANSWER: PAGE 115

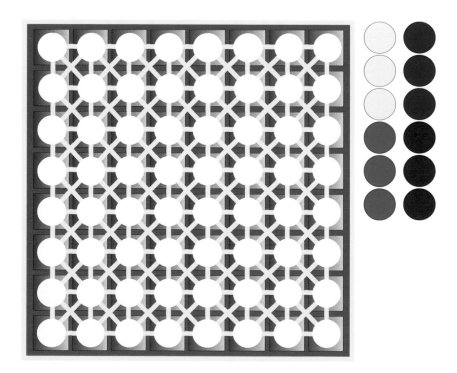

The king is the most important piece on the chess-board. If it is in any danger whatsoever it must be made safe. But what if several kings were pitted against each other? What would happen then?

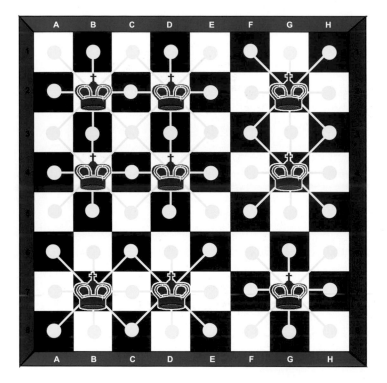

◀ KINGS' ATTACK

The smallest number of kings needed to attack all the unoccupied squares of a chessboard, without any of the kings being attacked by another, is nine kings as shown at left.

Can you work out how many kings are needed for a similar configuration in which every king is also under attack by another?

ANSWER: PAGE 116

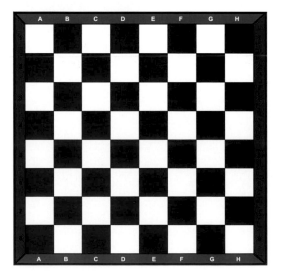

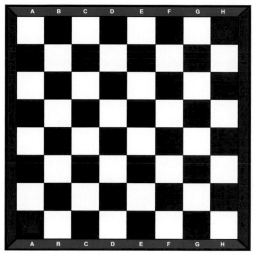

Puzzle 1

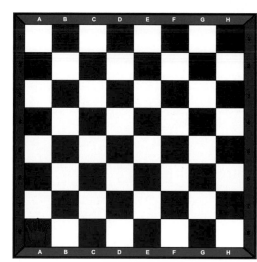

Puzzle 2

Puzzle 3

▶ QUEEN'S TOURS

Can you move a queen on a chessboard so that she visits all the squares of the board, according to the following rules:

Puzzle 1) What is the minimum number of moves required to visit all squares when squares are not allowed to be revisited? The starting and ending squares are shown.

Puzzle 2) What is the minimum number of moves required to achieve a closed tour (that is, with the tour ending on the square it started) when squares are allowed to be revisited?

Puzzle 3) Can you create a closed tour in which squares are not allowed to be revisited, and which has a fourfold rotational symmetry?

ANSWERS: PAGE 116

The diagonal movement of the bishop may appear more restricted than the king or queen, but just because it can only keep to one color square doesn't mean it should be underestimated.

Puzzle 1

Puzzle 2

▲ BISHOP'S TOURS

Bishops are restricted to diagonal movements only, and are confined to the squares of a single color of the gameboard.

So if a bishop starts on a black square he can only move to other black squares, moving in straight diagonal lines as far as he wishes. Even then, it is not possible to visit all the black squares of the board without revisiting some of them on the way.

PUZZLE 1

What is the largest number of squares that can be visited on a bishop's tour when squares are not allowed to be revisited?

The example shows a bishop's tour which left six black squares unvisited. Can you do better?

PUZZLE 2

What is the smallest number of moves in which a complete bishop's tour can be completed when squares are allowed to be revisited?

ANSWERS: PAGE 116

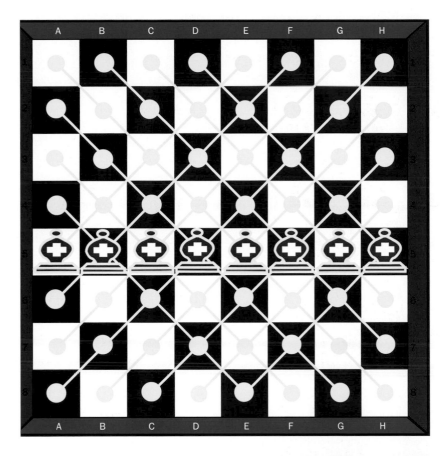

▶ BISHOPS ATTACKING

Eight bishops are needed to attack all the unoccupied squares of a chessboard.

None of the bishops is attacked by another, as shown above.

How many bishops are needed to create a configuration in which all squares are under attack and every bishop is also attacked by another?

ANSWER: PAGE 117

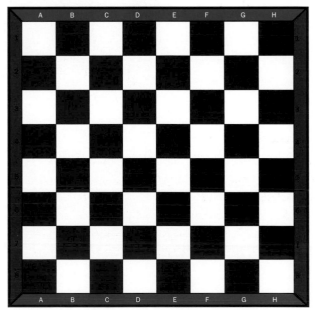

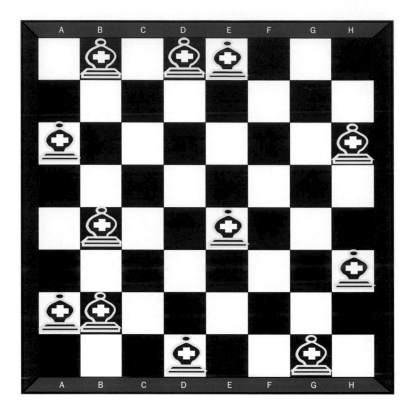

▲ BISHOPS NON-ATTACKING

What is the maximum number of bishops which can be placed on a chessboard so that none of them is under attack by another?

An arrangement of 12 bishops is shown above. Can you do better?

ANSWER: PAGE 117

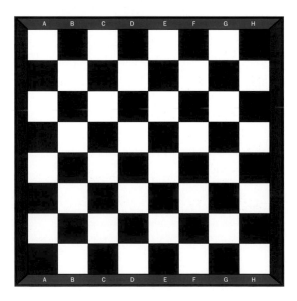

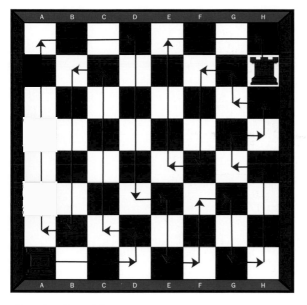

Puzzles 1 and 2

▼ ROOK'S TOURS

A rook's tour is a network in which the rook visits each square of the gameboard once and only once.

The rook moves horizontally or vertically as far as he likes.

What is the smallest (and the largest) number of moves for the rook to make a tour under the following conditions:

PUZZLES 1 AND 2

From a1 to h7 as shown. A 30-move solution is given. Can you do better for a minimal and maximal solution?

PUZZLES 3 AND 4

From a1 to a8 as shown. A 31-move solution is shown. Can you do better for a minimal and maximal solution?

PUZZLES 5 AND 6

A closed tour. A 20-move solution is shown. Can you do better for a minimal and maximal solution?

ANSWER: PAGE 117

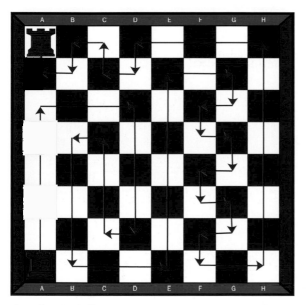

Puzzles 3 and 4

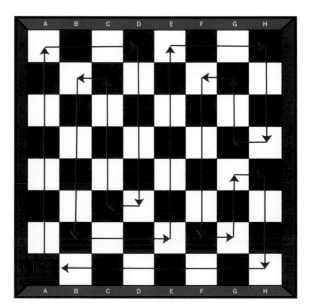

Puzzles 5 and 6

Whe is a knot not a knot? Can a mere tangle be called a potential knot—a knot-in-waiting perhaps? Let's hope such considerations don't have you up against the ropes.

▲ **LEONARDO'S KNOT**

How many threads were used by Leonardo to create the complex topological structure he used as his emblem? Leonardo's fascination with knots anticipated the modern interest in knots in topology and other sciences.

ANSWER: PAGE 118

▼ KNOT OR NOT?

Imagine the two dogs pulling the rope in different directions until it becomes a straight piece of rope.

Can you tell whether it will be a straight rope or a knotted one? If it will be knotted, how many knots will there be?

ANSWER: PAGE 118

✳ Knots

The topology of knots is not merely of interest to recreational and professional mathematicians. It has enormous importance in several other branches of science, particularly molecular biology. The structure of DNA molecules and those of complexly folded proteins have been elucidated with the help of the mathematical answer to the question: how does one untangle very long three-dimensional knots?

A single strand of human DNA can be as long as one meter. Coiled up, tightly interwoven, it fits in a cell nucleus having a diameter of about five millionths of a meter. And yet, when the DNA divides to make two identical copies of itself, these two copies slide apart in an effortless manner. What kind of knotting permits this smooth separation to happen? This is just one of the many questions that biologists face in their quest to understand the secrets of life itself, in which knots play such an important role.

Undoing and dealing with awkward knots requires careful observation and a lot of patience. See how you fare with the problems below. In the meantime, multicolored shoelaces anyone?

▲ KNOT COLORING

How many colors will be needed to color the five knots above according to the following coloring rules:

At each point where there is a crossing in the knot there are three areas to color:

1) The part that crosses over

2) One side of the strand underneath

3) The other side of the strand underneath.

At each crossing the strands should all be different colors, which means that the minimal number of colors required to color a knot is three.

These coloring rules are demonstrated by the colored knot 1.

ANSWER: PAGE 118

▲ **MORE KNOT COLORING**

How many colors will be needed to color the above knots according to the coloring rules given on the previous page?

ANSWER: PAGE 119

Knot problems might simply unravel in front of your eyes if you know the ropes. Just wait until you try to play with a dovetail joint—don't get stuck!

▲ PAPER KNOTS

Strips of paper are taped together forming knotlike structures.
   Which is the odd one out?

ANSWER: PAGE 120

▼ KNOTS PAIR

You can see two overhand knots of opposite handedness on a closed loop.
   Can they be removed from the loop—that is, cancel each other out?
   Can you exchange their positions on the loop?

ANSWER: PAGE 120

✳ Dovetail joints

The dovetail joint is an ancient way to make a rigid connection between two parts of wood without the use of screws, nails, or glue. The parts are joined by sliding the two pieces together as shown.

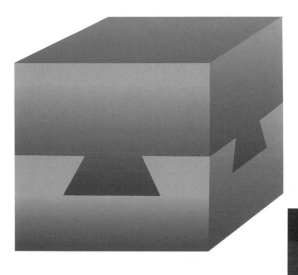

◀ IMPOSSIBLE DOVETAIL

How can you separate this seemingly impossible dovetail joint?

Unlike an ordinary dovetail, the four sides of this dovetail look the same.

ANSWER: PAGE 120

The four sides of the dovetail joint

Playing a agme against yourself can be fun—but if you're a team player, there's no reason why you can't play the same game and simply take turns.

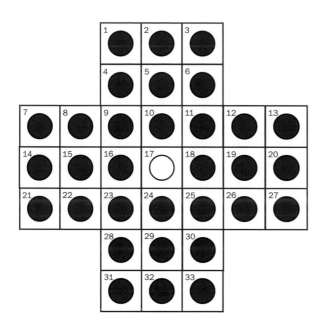

" **T**he game called Solitaire pleases me much.
Gottfried von Leibniz, in 1716 "

▲ PEG SOLITAIRE PUZZLE 1

Peg solitaire is one of the most popular single-person games. Its invention is attributed to a prisoner of the Bastille, in France.

There are many variations of the game, but the most popular by far is the one played on a board of 33 cells as shown.

The basic solitaire problem, and not an easy one, is one in which the counters are placed on all cells except the cell in the center (cell 17).

The object is to remove all pegs but one, in a series of jumps, ending with the last counter in the center cell.

A "jump" consists of moving a counter over any adjacent counter, removing it and landing on the next empty cell. One may jump vertically and horizontally but not diagonally. Each move must be a jump, and a chain of continuous jumps counts as one single move.

No one knows how many solutions exist. Obviously, 31 jumps are needed to get a solution, but taking chain jumps into consideration, the number of moves may be less than 31. The "world record" is a solution involving 18 moves, achieved by Ernest Bergholt in 1912.

In how many moves can you get a solution (or how far can you go before reaching a point at which no more jumps are possible)?

ANSWER: PAGE 120

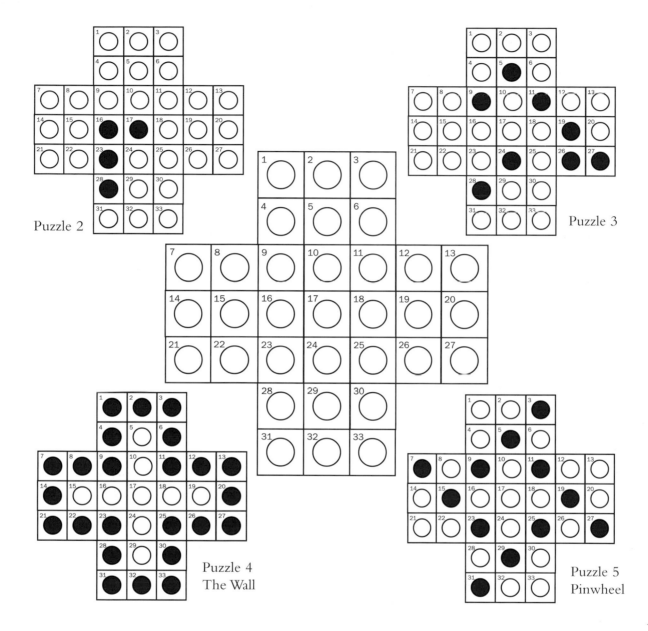

Puzzle 2

Puzzle 3

Puzzle 4
The Wall

Puzzle 5
Pinwheel

▲ PEG SOLITAIRE PUZZLES 2–5

What is the minimal number of moves to solve each of these classic puzzles?

PUZZLES 2 AND 3

Easier solitaire puzzles involve starting with a smaller number of counters, removing them as usual, and finishing in the center. Start with the patterns shown and land in the center with the last counter.

PUZZLES 4 AND 5

These are puzzles that start with a full board with the object of achieving a certain pattern formed by the remaining counters; some of these can be very difficult. For puzzles 4 and 5 start with the full board and stop when you have created the patterns shown.

ANSWERS: PAGE 121

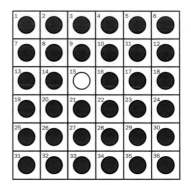

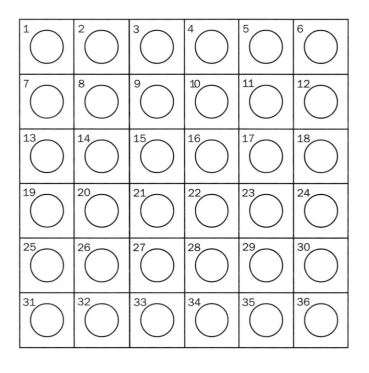

▲ SQUARE BOARD SOLITAIRE

Solitaire problems have been devised on boards other than the standard solitaire gameboard. Noble Carlson, an engineer from Ohio, posed the problem:

What is the smallest square solitaire board on which it is possible to start with a full board (except for an empty space at one of the corners) and end up with a single counter? It is not necessary for the counter to end in the space that was originally empty.

It has been shown that solutions are possible on all square boards that are multiples of three (except the 3-by-3 square).

Therefore the smallest solvable square board (for boards based on multiples of three) is the 6-by-6, although solving it is not an easy task.

Carlson found a solution requiring 29 moves, but John Harris of Santa Barbara, California, a reader of Martin Gardner's column, came up with a 15-move solution for all problems with non-corner starts.

In how many moves can you solve the 6-by-6 square board problem, starting with the empty space on square 15 (above)?

ANSWER: PAGE 121

▼ **GUITAR STRING**

A guitar string is stretched from point 1 to point 7 and marked at equal intervals.

Small folded pieces of paper are placed at 4, 5, and 6.

The string is pinched at 3 and twanged at 2.

What happens to the papers?

ANSWER: PAGE 122

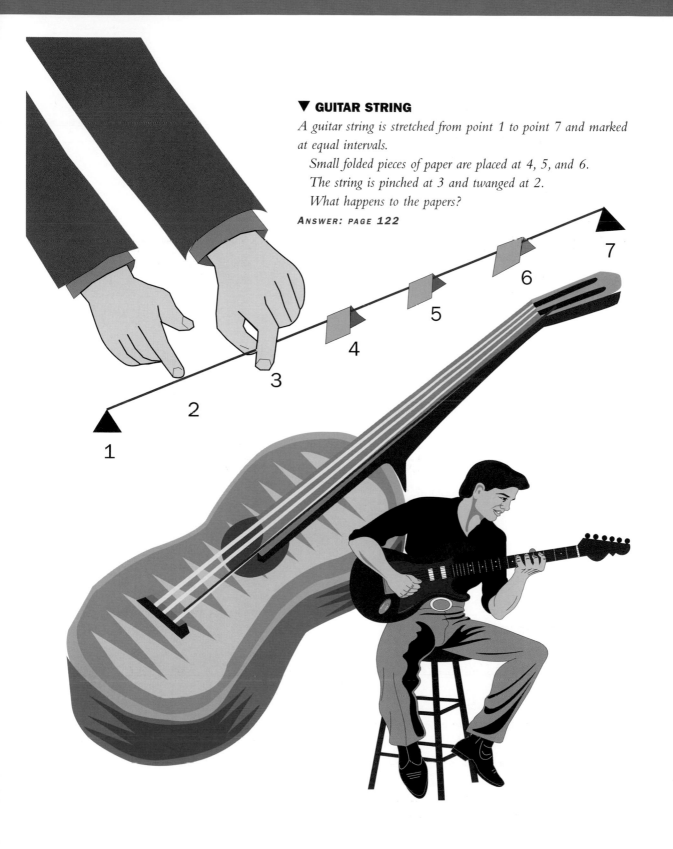

Whether tiling the bathroom or pasting up wallpaper, there's a lot of symmetry involved in matching up patterns while decorating. Of course, you could just use paint, but who wants to look at plain walls?

▲ HEXAGONAL NON-MATCHING PUZZLE

Arrange these seven tiles to form a single shape whereby these two conditions hold:
a) Where two edges meet, they must be of different colors.
b) The outline of the overall shape must be symmetrical.

ANSWER: PAGE 122

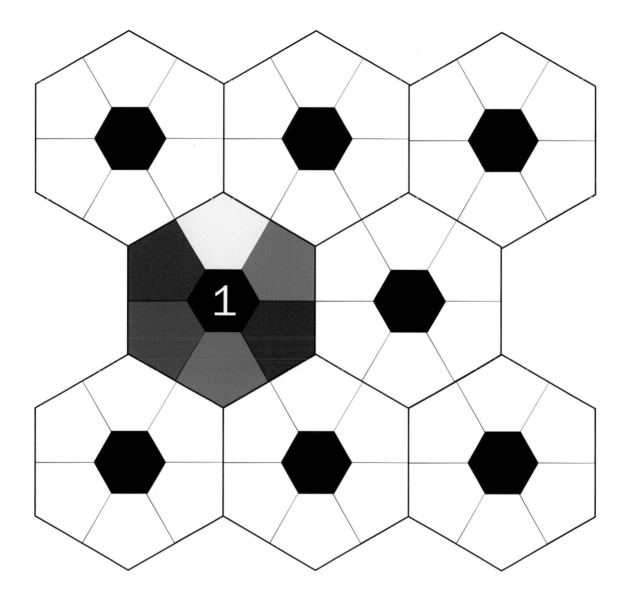

▲ HEXAGON MATCH

The vertices of each of the hexagons in the honeycomb tessellation above are to be colored in six different colors, the same six colors used for each hexagon, as shown in the colored hexagon above.

How many different colorings will you need to color the whole honeycomb so that all touching vertices match in color, domino-style?

Rotations and mirror images of a pattern are considered to be identical.

ANSWER: PAGE 122

When a queen is on the prowl on the chessboard, it's almost impossible to escape. When multiple queens are on the loose, things become even trickier.

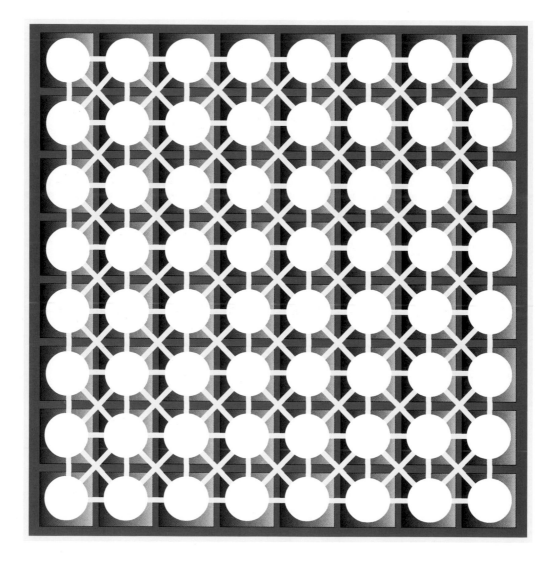

▲ QUEENS' ATTACK 1

What is the smallest number of chess queens required to keep all the squares of an 8-by-8 chessboard under attack (including the squares occupied by the queens themselves)?

ANSWER: PAGE 123

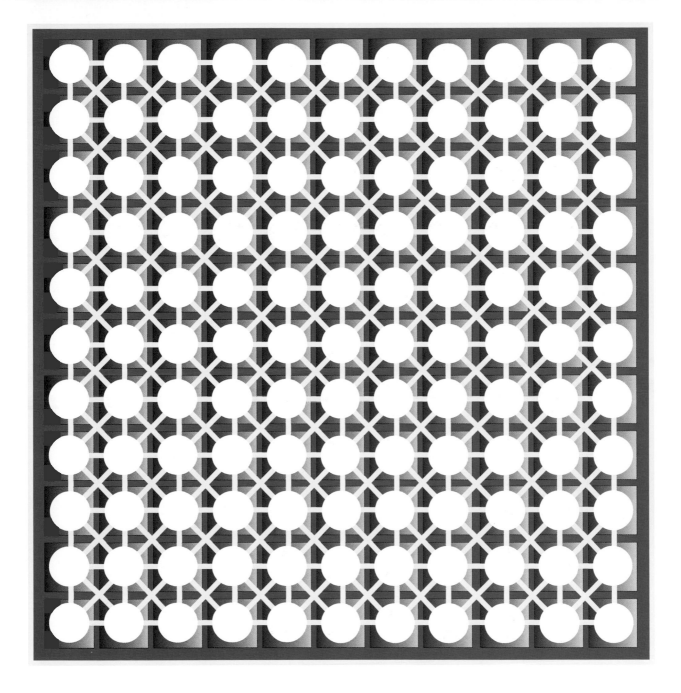

▲ QUEENS' ATTACK 2

What is the smallest number of chess queens required to keep all the squares of an 11-by-11 chessboard under attack (this time excluding the squares occupied by the queens themselves)?

ANSWER: PAGE 123

Trial and error is one way of solving a puzzle but logic is a far more powerful method. Think carefully and use your common sense while figuring out how you might identify the false coin below.

▲ WEIGHING EIGHT COINS

We have eight gold coins, one of which is false. The false coin is lighter than the rest, which are all of equal weight.

What is the minimal number of weighings on the scale (weighing only coins against other coins) required to be assured of finding the false coin?

ANSWER: PAGE 124

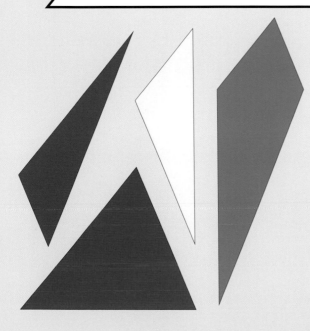

▲ TRIANGLES IN A TRIANGLE

Copy and cut out three copies of the set of four shapes at left.

From the three sets of four shapes can you form three different triangles that can then be put together to form the large triangle above?

ANSWER: PAGE 125

These puzzles are harder versions of the puzzles on page 23. Try them if you dare.

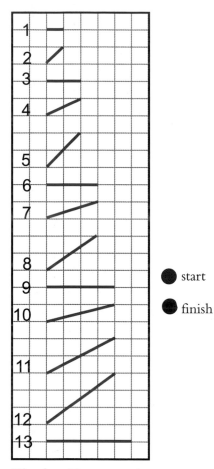

The first 13 consecutive moves

● start

● finish

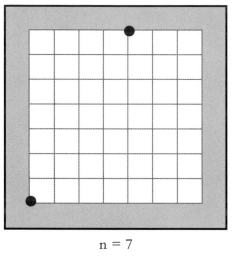

n = 7

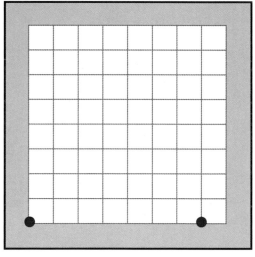

n = 8

MORE SQUARE ROUTES

Starting from a chosen point, consecutive lengths are added as shown in the examples above.

The object of the game is to draw as many consecutive lengths as possible and finish the line at a given end point.

The line may not cross itself.

Solutions are given for n = 2, 3, and 4 on page 23. Can you find the best solutions (the longest possible line) for n = 7 and n = 8?

ANSWER: PAGE 125

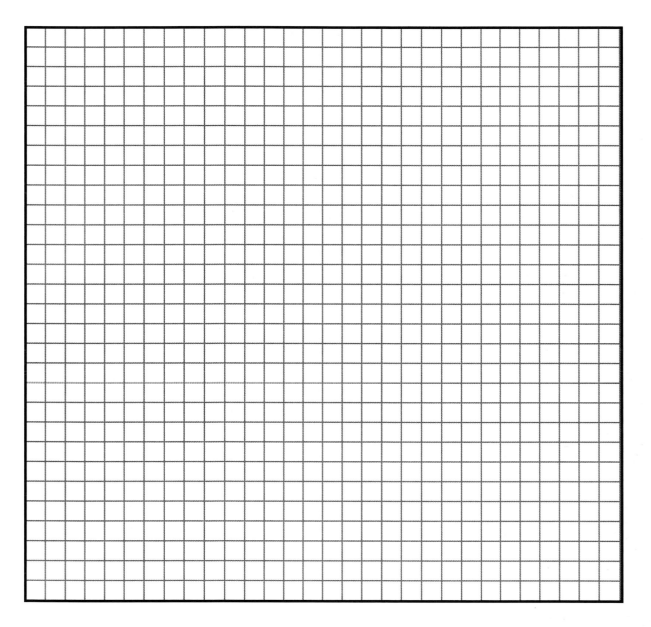

1 x 2
1 x 3
1 x 4

The first three
rectangles

▲ CONSECUTIVE RECTANGLES

*Using consecutive integers from 1 to 9, paired up as the dimensions
of a rectangle, each pair once, how many different rectangles can you create,
excluding squares? (There are 36 different rectangles.)*

*Can you place them all without overlap to cover a 29-by-30 rectangle?
If not, how much of the rectangle can you cover?*

ANSWER: PAGE 126

Amathematical series sounds like it ought to be on television—but what kind of show would it be? Maybe an algebraic cop show with a good equation/bad equation situation? Then again, maybe not.

▲ PARALLELOGRAM OF VARIGNON

We have three randomly drawn quadrilaterals.

The sides of the one at top left are bisected and the four points joined, forming a parallelogram.

Its sides are parallel to the two diagonals of the original quadrilateral.

Can you work out the relationships of the area of this parallelogram to the area of the quadrilateral and of the perimeter of the parallelogram to the main diagonals of the quadrilaterals?

Will a similar construction with other quadrilaterals result in a parallelogram? Try it with the two given quadrilaterals.

ANSWER: PAGE 127

1

1/2

1/4

1/8

1/16

1/32

1/64

1/128

1/256

1/512

▲ MATHEMATICAL SERIES

Above, a geometric series is demonstrated visualizing the first 10 terms of the following series:

$$1 + \frac{1}{2} + \frac{1}{4} + \frac{1}{8} + \frac{1}{16} + \frac{1}{32} + \frac{1}{64} + \frac{1}{128} + \frac{1}{256} + \frac{1}{512} + \ldots + \frac{1}{2^n} + \ldots$$

What is the limit of the geometric series as n approaches infinity?

Below, another mathematical series (a harmonic series) is visualized, again for its first 10 terms:

$$1 + \frac{1}{2} + \frac{1}{3} + \frac{1}{4} + \frac{1}{5} + \frac{1}{6} + \frac{1}{7} + \frac{1}{8} + \frac{1}{9} + \frac{1}{10} + \ldots + \frac{1}{n} + \ldots$$

What is the limit of the harmonic series as n approaches infinity?
What is the difference between the two mathematical series?

ANSWER: PAGE 127

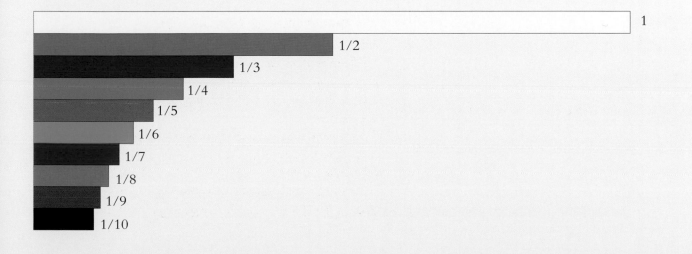

1

1/2

1/3

1/4

1/5

1/6

1/7

1/8

1/9

1/10

Number sequences are all around us and are how we make sense of the world. How else would we find an address for the first time or drift to sleep while counting sheep?

1	11	95	33	59	58	28	54	13	100	
38	36	18	69	98	49	17	16	41	96	
60	32	40	4	67	9	92	23	30	15	
57	19	2	39	3	85	29	55	34	47	
52	27	22	76	42	62	7	43	99	93	
91	51	48	21	77	80	72	50	79	45	
89	20	75	46	35	31	44	94	56	84	
61	8	6	90	74	25	10	64	78	86	
73	87	101	88	83	82	26	81	97	71	
63	37	68	12	70	53	66	24	14	65	5

◄ NUMBER SEQUENCE 101

Can you arrange the first 101 integers in the table at left in such a way as to avoid an increasing or decreasing sequence of 11 integers (starting at the top and reading from left to right)?

The sequence of 11 increasing or decreasing integers doesn't have to be consecutive; it can be randomly spaced throughout the table.

An increasing sequence of 11 integers was not avoided; one of many is shown in red.

Can you do better?

To spare you a futile exercise, it is a proven fact that no matter how you arrange the 101 integers, you will inevitably always be able to find 11 integers in an increasing or decreasing sequence.

Now take only 100 integers and try again to arrange them in such a way as to avoid creating an increasing or decreasing sequence of 11 integers.

Can it be done?

ANSWER: PAGE 128

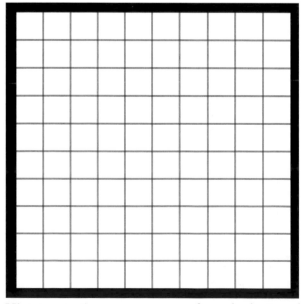

Hint: try starting your sequence from the bottom left.

▼ NUMBER PARTITIONING

Godfrey Hardy and Srinivasa Ramanujan's famous joint paper dealt with the theory of partitions—the ways of representing a given whole number n as the sum of positive whole numbers.

For example, the number 5 can be "partitioned" in seven ways as shown below.

Can you work out in how many ways you can partition the numbers 6 and 10?

ANSWER: PAGE 128

5	=	5					
5	=	4	+	1			
5	=	3	+	2			
5	=	3	+	1	+	1	
5	=	2	+	2	+	1	
5	=	2	+	1	+	1	+	1
5	=	1	+	1	+	1	+	1	+	1

Tiling is easy when the pieces are all the same shape and fit snugly onto the gameboard. But it gets more complicated when the tiles varying sizes. For example, which piece do you start with?

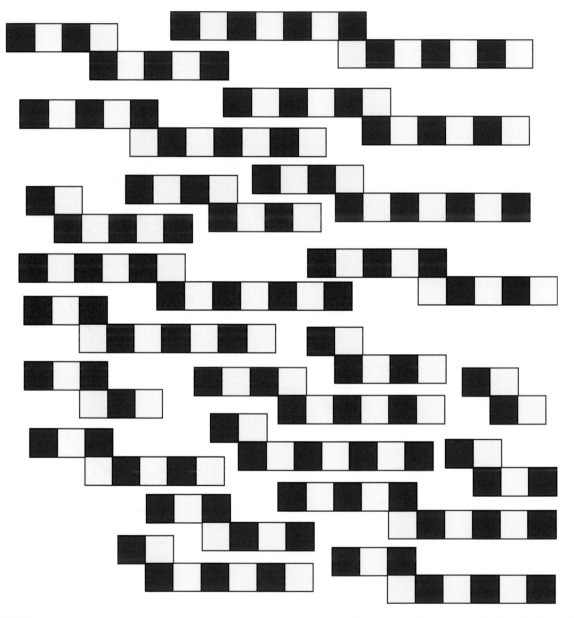

▲ ZIGTILES

Zigtiles are related to polyominoes.

Can you discover the logic of their growth and find the next shape in the sequence (currently missing)? Note that the pieces are not presented in sequence.

As a puzzle, can you determine whether all pieces (including the missing piece) can be fitted on the gameboard?

As a two-person game, players choose a color and take turns placing a tile, trying to join squares of their color. The winner is the player with the greatest number of joined squares of his or her color.

ANSWER: PAGE 122

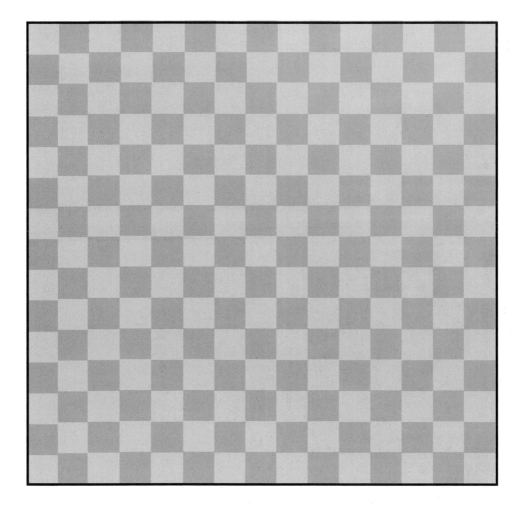

Zigtiles gameboard

▼ MONDRIAN GALLERY (page 7)

Black–and–white Mondrian: the real Mondrian is the lower left composition. It is titled "Composition With Lines" from 1917.

The subjectively "best" picture in the experiment was found to be the upper right composition.

Color Mondrian: the real Mondrian is the first painting.

▼ MINIMAL ART (page 8)

Just one single element was used to create the artworks.

Each of the compositions was created from the same number of identical elements, each appearing in one of four possible orientations.

A hundred years ago Pere Dominique Donat introduced the idea that "an infinity of different patterns could be produced from a small number of basic elements by permutations and symmetries."

In 1922, Andreas Speiser published the "Theory of Groups of Finite Order," in which he analyzed ornaments of ancient civilizations, finding that there was no known mathematics in which he could formulate their complexity. Here it was not mathematics that produced art, but rather art that produced mathematics. Speiser started with the elementary operations of symmetry, translation, rotation, and reflection, from which he obtained complexities (that is, groups of all operations of symmetry by combinations: 17 groups altogether, by means of which he could mathematically describe all conceivable ornaments).

▼ MINIMAL STRIPS (page 9)

There are 64 different patterns that can be made by joining three squares in a row.

▼ PERCEPT (page 10)

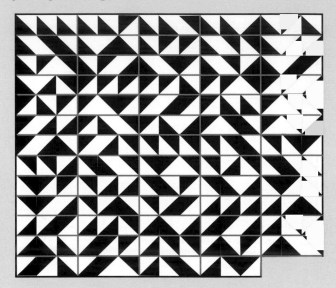

▼ **LOOKING AT CATS AND MICE (page 11)**

It is impossible to add a cat and two mice on the gameboard.

▼ **MORE CATS AND MICE (page 11)**

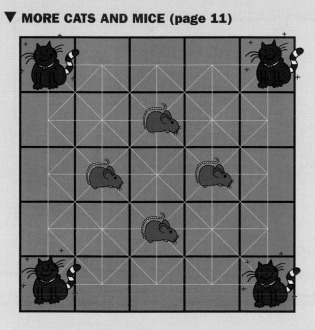

▼ **HEXABITS 1—I CHING (page 12)**

▼ **HEXABITS 2—YIN AND YANG (page 13)**

One of the many solutions.

▼ **EXACT NEGATIVES (page 14)**

Mask B creates the exact negative in each case.

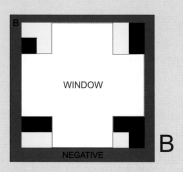

▼ POOL ACCIDENT (page 15)

If the ball sinks to the bottom of the pool, it will displace water equal to its own volume.

If the ball falls into the boat, it will displace water equal to its own weight (this is Archimedes' Principle). Since it is reasonable to assume that the bowling ball is denser than the water, this method will displace the greater amount of water.

▼ COLORING SQUARES PUZZLES 1 AND 2 (page 16)

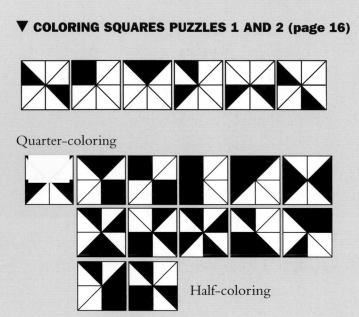

Quarter-coloring

Half-coloring

▼ BINARY PATTERN (page 17)

Four moves are necessary: rows 1 and 4, and columns 2 and 3.

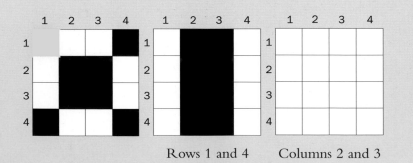

Rows 1 and 4   Columns 2 and 3

▼ BEADS AND NECKLACES (page 18)

There are only be three basic patterns; substitution of colors creates 12 distinct necklaces as shown.

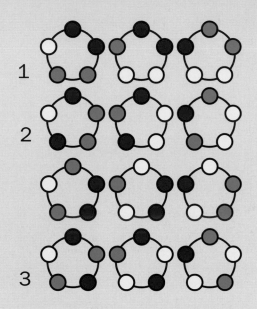

▼ PAIRING NECKLACE (page 19)

A necklace consisting of only 16 beads can fulfill the objective, as shown.

In general a "universal cycle for 2-sequences" exists for any collection of n colors; the cycle has length n^2.

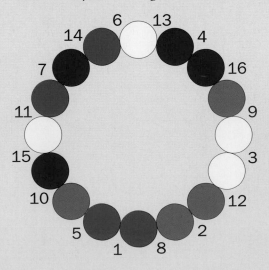

▼ **ANAGRAM 1 (page 20)**
RANGE and ANGER

▶ **HEXAGON LOOP (page 22)**

▼ **ANAGRAM 2 (page 20)**
SAUCER

▼ **WORD STRIPS (page 21)**

The 5-letter words:

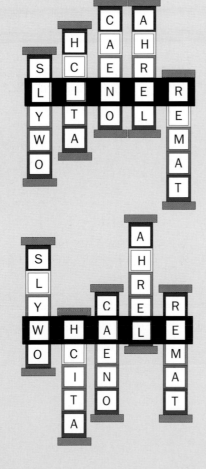

LACER	SHEET	STOAT
SACRA	SHOAT	STOLE
SANER	SHOER	STORE
SCALE	SHORT	STORM
SCARE	STALE	WHEAT
SCORE	STARE	WHELM
SHALE	START	WHERE
SHALT	STEAM	WHOLE
SHARE	STEER	WHORE
SHEAR	STELA	YACHT
SHEER	STELE	

▼ SQUARE ROUTES (page 23)

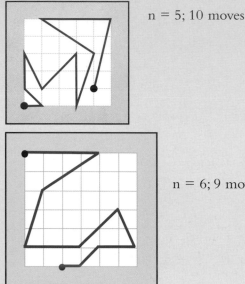

n = 5; 10 moves

n = 6; 9 moves

▼ SIPHON SYSTEMS (page 24)

The model demonstrates the operation principle of the intermittent siphon.

The water will first slowly fill the lower middle compartment until the water level reaches the top of the bent tube, which will start the operation of the siphon, quickly emptying the middle compartment. The cycle starts again until the upper compartment is emptied.

Why?

The weight of the liquid is greater in the longer arm of the siphon, which makes it flow until the compartment is empty.

The basic condition for the siphon to operate is that the discharge end must be lower than the intake end.

The action of the siphon has been known to engineers for many centuries. It has had many and varied uses. One of the best examples of the use of the principle of the siphon is found in the Fountain with Automata of Ramelli (1531-1604), constructed during the Renaissance. It was a complex arrangement of pipes and siphons with counterweights that made mechanical birds sing and flutter their wings, all by the action of water. One later, more practical application of the siphon is in the flushing of a toilet.

The general study of the siphon in engineering is contained in the field of hydrokinetics, which is a branch of hydrodynamics.

The model can be reset for a new demonstration simply by inverting it again.

▼ COLOR CRYPTOGRAM (page 25)

"There is no substitute for hard work"
—Thomas Edison.

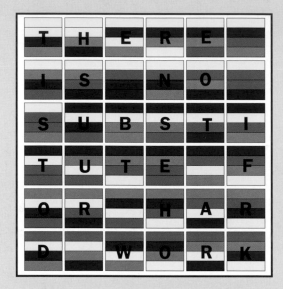

▼ CHAIN BALANCE (page 26)

The chain from the filled tray will start "flowing" to the lower compartment as long as this arm is longer than the other arm, simply because it is heavier.

The "chain siphon" is a partial mechanical analogue of the operating principle of the siphon.

This mechanical demonstration, of course, does not involve the function of a vacuum, nor air pressure. The model demonstrates only the idea of the difference in the length of the arms.

▶ **TREASURE CHESTS (page 27)**
The password is CREATIVITY.

▼ **TOPOLOGICAL TRANSFORMATION (page 28)**

The basic concepts of topology include many ideas we learn as infants: insideness and outsideness, right- and left-handedness, linking, knotting, connectedness and disconnectedness.

Most topological experiments are based on transformations, that is, changes in the shape of a surface without any breaking. Two figures are said to be topologically equivalent if one can be continuously deformed into another. So a sphere and a cube are topologically equivalent, and the figure 8 and letter B are topologically equivalent (each has two holes). A fundamental problem in topology is to classify objects into classes of topologically equivalent things.

Topologists have been called mathematicians who don't know the difference between a mug of coffee and a doughnut (the two being topologically equivalent).

▶ **ALPHABET LOGIC (page 29)**
The letters should be placed as shown at right. The odd ones out are in red.

MVCN LW

No curved lines; can be drawn with a single line

FOGT USJ

No enclosed areas

DQYP AR

Enclosed areas

▶ **PINWHEEL FOLDS (page 30)**

The sequence of folding the flaps:

3 – 8 – 1 – 10 – 5 – 7 – 4 – 6 – 2 – 9

◀ **FIFTH COLOR (page 31)**

McGregor's map was, of course, an April Fool's Day joke.

The four-color theorem was proved in 1976, stating that for any map in the plane, four colors are sufficient to color it.

After the publication of this puzzle, Martin Gardner received hundreds of letters with the map colored with four colors; one such solution is shown at left.

▼ FOUR-COLOR CROSSING (page 32)
An example of a winning line is shown.

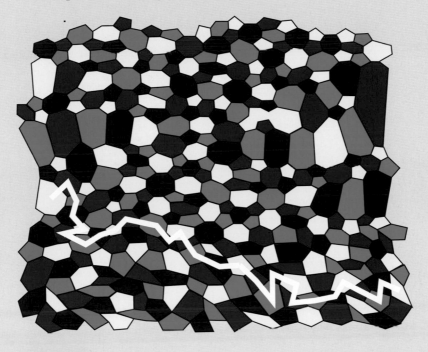

▼ COLORING PATTERNS (page 33)
Both diagrams can be completely colored using three colors.

▶ M-PIRE PROBLEM (page 34)

It is interesting to note that each 2–pire touches all the other colors, proving that 12 colors are necessary.

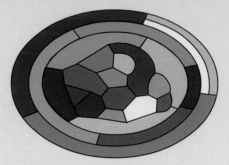

▼ SNARKS (page 35)

Four colors are required (as shown). Martin Gardner gave the name "snarks" to graphs that cannot be completed with three colors so that no two lines of the same color will meet at any junction (node).

Technically, these are called "uncolorable trivalent graphs."

The work on such graphs was started by Rufus Isaacs of Johns Hopkins University in 1975.

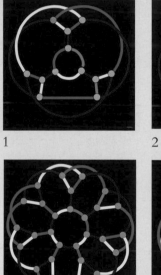

1

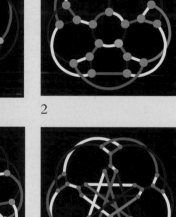

2

3

4

✳ Edge coloring of graphs

The problem of edge coloring of graphs arises in a great variety of scheduling applications, typically associated with minimizing the number of noninterfering rounds needed to complete a given set of tasks.

For example, consider a situation where we need to schedule a given set of two-person interviews. We can construct a graph in which the vertices represent people and the edges connect the pairs of people who want to meet. An edge coloring of the graph defines the schedule. The colors represent the different time periods, with all meetings of the same color happening simultaneously.

The minimum number of colors needed to edge-color a graph is known as the edge-chromatic number or chromatic index.

▼ CENTER POINT (page 36)

The fourth point from the left.

▼ MY CENTIPEDE (page 36)

The central horizontal lines are all of equal lengths.

▼ VERTICAL SWORDS (page 37)

Look at the page with your eyes close to the level of the paper from a point at the lower right of the page.

▼ INTERRUPTED CIRCLES (page 38)

The red circle.

▼ **INTERRUPTED LINES (page 39)**
The green lines.

▼ **MÖBIUS STRIP BISECTED (page 40)**
It will stay in one piece of twice the length and having two complete twists.

The edges are now two separate curves, linked to each other but not individually knotted.

▼ **MÖBIUS STRIP TRISECTED (page 40)**
Two linked strips, one of them a Möbius strip of the same length, the other a strip of twice the length with two complete twists.

▼ **SIAMESE MÖBIUS STRIP (page 41)**
The result will be an interesting structure, consisting of one piece with two sides, three edges, no twists, and two holes.

Topologically speaking, the twist in the upper part gets canceled out by the one in the lower part.

▼ **MÖBIUS PAIRS (page 42)**

1 and 2) The unexpected outcome will be a square ring with two sides, two edges, and zero twists.

3) If both strips are the same handedness, you get two separate skeletal sphere quadrants, both with two sides, two edges; one twisted, the other not. If the strips are of different handedness, you get two linked skeletal sphere quadrants; both twisted.

▼ **MÖBIUS NESTED PAIRS (page 43)**
1) Four separate identical skeletal sphere quadrants with two sides, two edges, and zero twists.
2) Two separate identical skeletal sphere quadrants with two sides, two edges, and zero twists and one twisted loop with two edges and two sides.
3) If both strips are the same handedness, you get two separate skeletal sphere quadrants, both with two sides, two edges; one small untwisted, the other long and twisted. If the strips are of different handedness, you get one small seperate skeletal sphere quadrant untwisted; one seperate two-sided, untwisted hexagonal ring.

▼ **SLOTTED RING (page 44)**
The result will be a chain of three interlinked links, two rings, and one Möbius strip.

▼ **BELT DRIVE (page 45)**

A cylindrical strip of paper can be stretched between two cylindrical rollers. A Möbius strip can be stretched between three as shown in our belt drive.

The one-sidedness of the Möbius strip was exploited by the B.F. Goodrich company, who patented conveyor belts that last twice as long as conventional belts by uniformly spreading wear on both sides of the belt.

▶ **MÖBIUS OR NOT? (page 46)**

The outcome of bisecting Manning's surface is a plane square ring, with two edges, two sides, and zero twist. (It is therefore not equivalent to a Möbius strip, which would result in a different shape if bisected.)

▼ **REGULAR POLYHEDRA RINGS (page 47)**

Kurth Schucker found out that rings could be made by joining eight identical units of any of the regular polyhedra along their faces, except the tetrahedron.

No matter how many tetrahedrons are joined along their faces, no rings are possible.

Proof of this was provided by J.H. Mason in 1972.

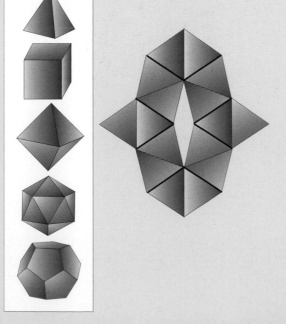

▼ **HOPSTIX (page 49)**

The multiple jump of the circles player puts him or her in a winning position. In three more moves it is a win.

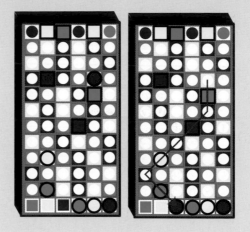

▼ **HEX GAME (page 50)**

An opening move of 1D, 2C, 3B, or 4A will give a win to the first player in 7 moves.

The first player can win on a 5-by-5 gameboard if he plays in the middle cell on his first move.

On larger gameboards the situation becomes more complex, and on an 11-by-11 gameboard an enormous number of game situations are possible. It is interesting to note that although there is no specific procedure found to ensure a win, there exists a proof that a winning strategy exists for the first player on a board of any size.

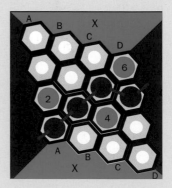

▼ KNIGHTS' BLACK ATTACK (page 53)

Seven knights are sufficient, as shown.

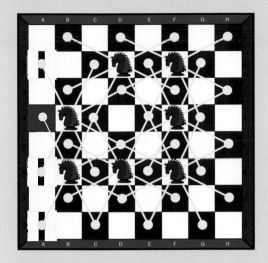

▼ KNIGHTS' AVOIDANCE (page 53)

Since knights change the color of the square they land on each time they move, you can place 32 knights on white squares (or black squares), none of them attacked by another.

▼ KNIGHTS' ALL-OUT ATTACK 1 (page 54)

14 knights are needed as shown below.

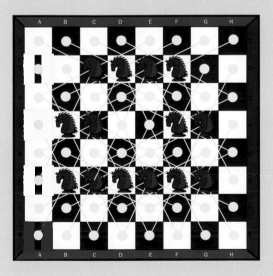

▼ KNIGHTS' ALL-OUT ATTACK 2 (page 55)

14 knights are needed, as shown below.

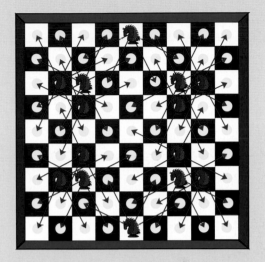

▼ KNIGHTS' ALL-OUT ATTACK 3 (page 55)

16 knights are needed, as shown below.

▼ **KNIGHT'S TOURS—UNCROSSED (page 56)**

Puzzle 1
3-by-3 gameboard;
2 moves.

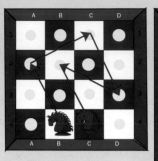

Puzzle 2
4-by-4 gameboard;
5 moves.

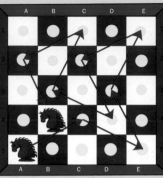

Puzzle 3
5-by-5 gameboard;
10 moves.

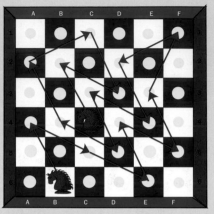

Puzzle 4
6-by-6 gameboard; 17 moves.

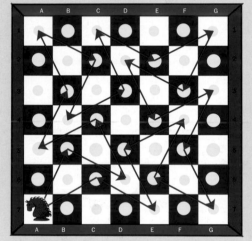

Puzzle 5
7-by-7 gameboard; 24 moves (closed tour).

Puzzle 6
8-by-8 gameboard; 35 moves.

▼ **KNIGHT'S TOURS—CROSSED**
(page 57)

A knight's tour is impossible on the 3-by-3 and 4-by-4 boards.
The 5-by-5 and 6-by-6 boards have 128 and 320 different tours,
some of them closed. The total number of tours on the 7-by-7
board is over 7,000, while the number of tours on the 8-by-8
board is in the millions.

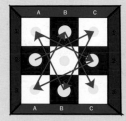

Puzzle 1
3-by-3 gameboard

Puzzle 2
4-by-4 gameboard

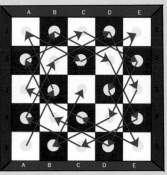

Puzzle 3
5-by-5 gameboard

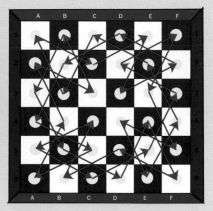

Puzzle 4
6-by-6 gameboard (closed tour)

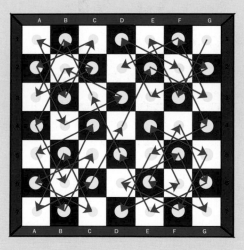

Puzzle 5
7-by-7 gameboard

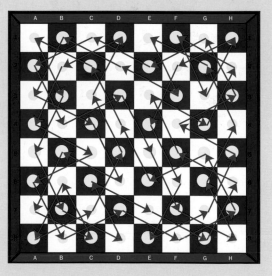

Puzzle 6
8-by-8 gameboard (closed tour)

▼ LENSES (page 58)

The rays will converge more than with one lens. The second lens bends the light more, so the total bend is larger.

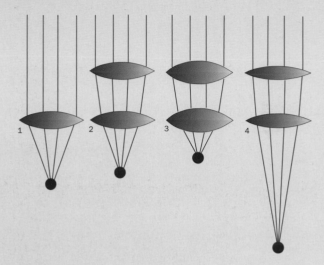

▼ BURNING LENSES (page 59)

Lens 2 is thicker than lens 1 and therefore will bend the light the most, producing a smaller image of the sun.

Lenses 3 and 4 are negative lenses and will not cause the sunlight to converge at all, so they cannot burn the paper.

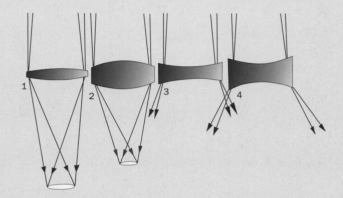

▼ LIGHT REFLECTION (page 60)

Hero of Alexandria discovered that a beam of light directed towards a mirror or any other reflecting surface at an angle will bounce off at an equal angle (the angle of incidence) to the angle of reflection.

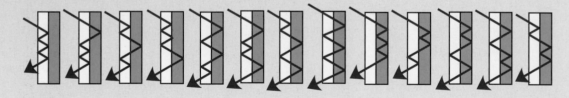

▶ GOLDFISH (page 61)

Without water the fish would occupy the small angle S but with water the light is refracted (bent) and the fish seems to occupy the large angle L and will also seem to be nearer the surface than it really is.

Light travels at different speeds through different substances. It travels more slowly in water than it does through air, and it also changes direction. This is called refraction; rays bend at the point where the two substances meet.

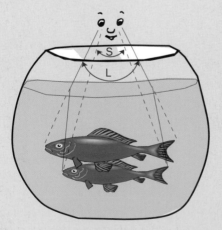

▼ THE EIGHT QUEENS PROBLEM (page 62)

The twelve solutions for the standoff are shown below.

▼ **QUEENS' MINI STANDOFF (page 64)**

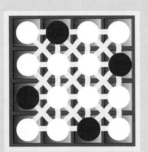

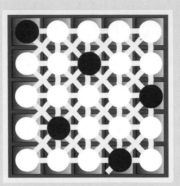

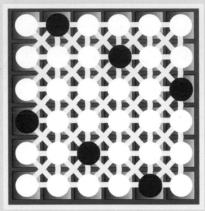

Puzzle 1
(one of two possible
solutions)

Puzzle 2
(one of ten possible
solutions)

Puzzle 3
(one of four possible
solutions)

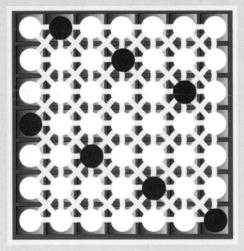

Puzzle 4
(one of seven possible solutions)

▼ **QUEENS' COLOR STANDOFF 1 (page 65)**

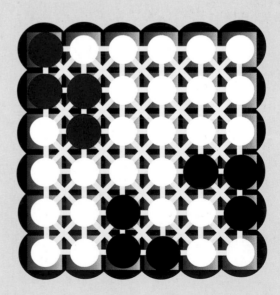

▼ QUEENS' COLOR STANDOFF 2 AND 3 (page 66)

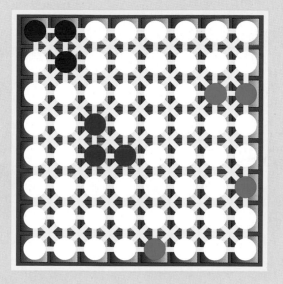 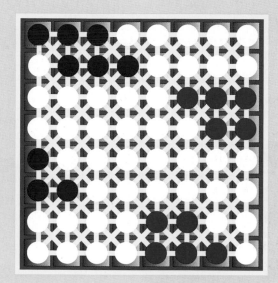

▼ QUEENS' COLOR STANDOFF 4 AND 5 (page 67)

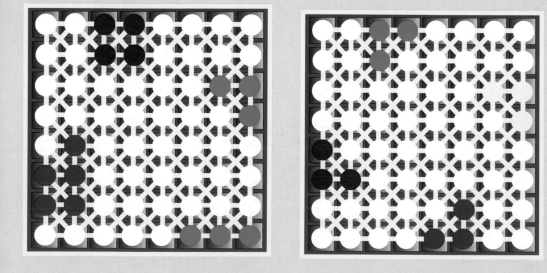

▼ KINGS' ATTACK (page 68)

12 kings are needed so that every square is under attack, including occupied squares.

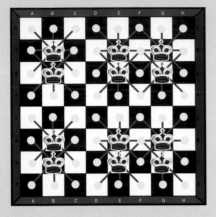

▼ QUEENS' TOURS (page 69)

Puzzle 1—a 15-move solution

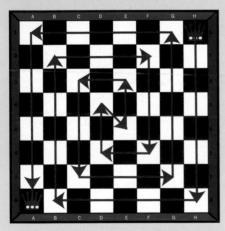

Puzzle 2—a 14-move solution.

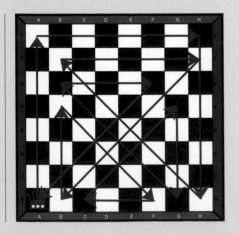

▼ QUEENS' TOURS (continued)

Puzzle 3—a closed tour with fourfold rotational symmetry. Others solutions are possible.

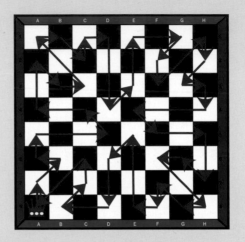

▼ BISHOP'S TOURS (page 70)

PUZZLE 1

The best that can be achieved by a bishop's tour when squares are not allowed to be revisited is 29 black squares.

No matter how you move the bishop, there will always be at least three unvisited black squares.

PUZZLE 2

If we allow the bishop to revisit squares, it is possible to visit every black square. Starting at one corner and ending in the opposite corner, this can be done in a tour of 17 moves, as shown.

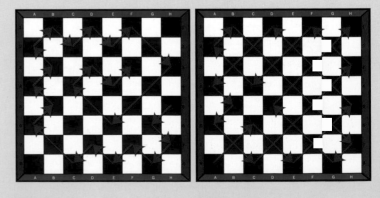

PUZZLE 1   PUZZLE 2

▼ BISHOPS ATTACKING (page 71)

Ten bishops are needed.

▼ BISHOPS NON-ATTACKING (page 72)

The maximum number of bishops that can be placed on a chessboard without any being attacked is 14, as shown.

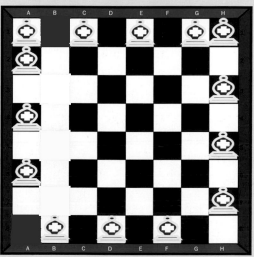

▼ ROOK'S TOURS (page 73)

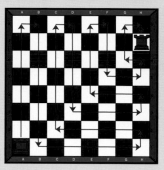
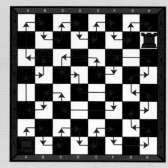

PUZZLE 1

Minimal solution: 21 moves.

PUZZLE 2

Maximal solution: 55 moves.

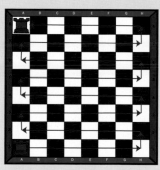
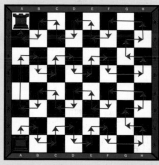

PUZZLE 3

Minimal solution: 15 moves.

PUZZLE 4

Maximal solution: 57 moves.

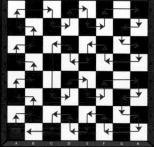

PUZZLE 5

Minimal solution: 16 moves.

PUZZLE 6

Maximal solution: 56 moves.

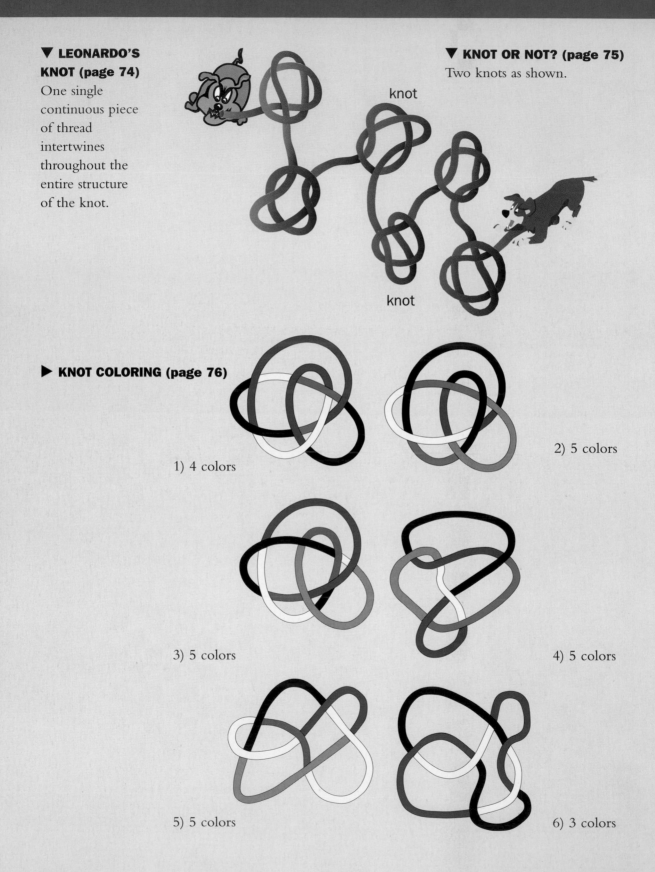

▼ **LEONARDO'S KNOT (page 74)**
One single continuous piece of thread intertwines throughout the entire structure of the knot.

▼ **KNOT OR NOT? (page 75)**
Two knots as shown.

knot

knot

▶ **KNOT COLORING (page 76)**

1) 4 colors

2) 5 colors

3) 5 colors

4) 5 colors

5) 5 colors

6) 3 colors

▼ **MORE KNOT COLORING (page 77)**

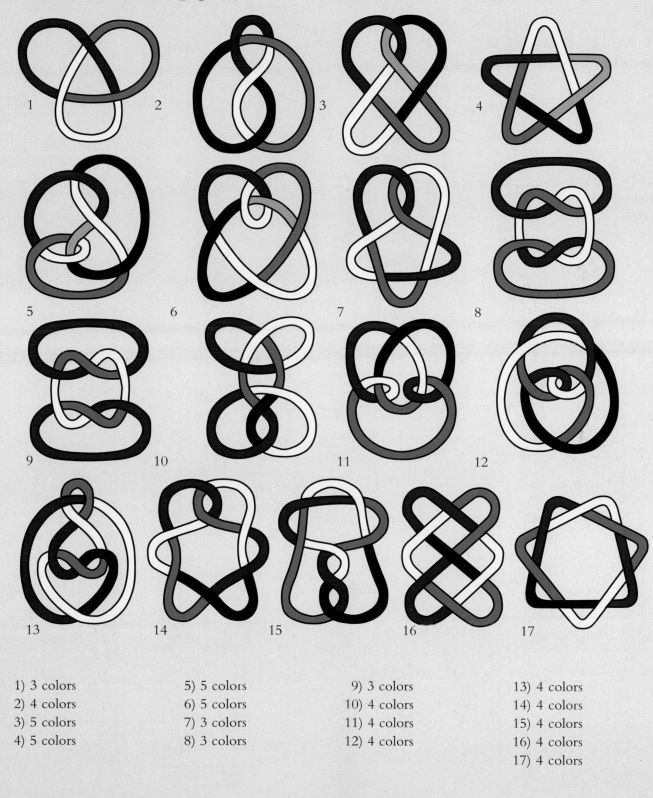

1) 3 colors
2) 4 colors
3) 5 colors
4) 5 colors

5) 5 colors
6) 5 colors
7) 3 colors
8) 3 colors

9) 3 colors
10) 4 colors
11) 4 colors
12) 4 colors

13) 4 colors
14) 4 colors
15) 4 colors
16) 4 colors
17) 4 colors

▼ PAPER KNOTS (page 78)

All are single knots except 4, which consists of two linked knots.

▼ KNOTS PAIR (page 78)

The two knots cannot be removed from the loop, but one can go through the other to the other side, preserving both knots' handedness.

▶ IMPOSSIBLE DOVETAIL (page 79)

A classic puzzle

The two blocks are joined by two angled dovetails. They slide along the diagonal to separate.

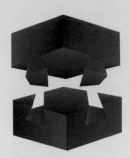

▼ PEG SOLITAIRE PUZZLE 1 (page 80)

Here's Ernest Bergholt's 18-move solution

That 18 is the minimal solution has been proved by John Beasley of Cambridge University.

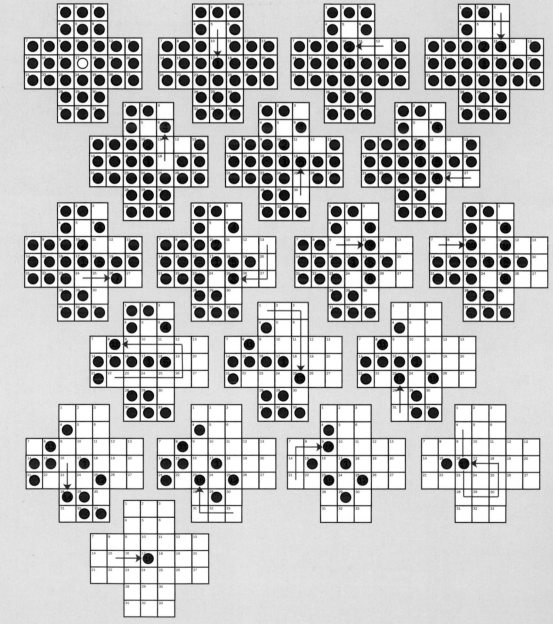

▼ **PEG SOLITAIRE PUZZLES 2–5 (page 81)**

PUZZLE 2

Three moves: 17–15, 28–16, 15–17.

PUZZLE 3

Three moves: 27–25–23, 26–16–4–6–18, 19–17.

PUZZLE 4: THE WALL

Six moves: 5–17; 24–10; 32–24; 19–17–29; 15–17; 10–24–32.

PUZZLE 5: PINWHEEL

20 moves: 29–17; 22–24; 17–29; 15–17; 4–16; 17–15; 5–17; 12–10; 17–5; 19–17; 30–18; 17–19; 31–23; 33–31; 7–9; 21–7; 3–11; 1–3; 27–25; 13–27.

▼ **SQUARE BOARD SOLITAIRE (page 82)**

John Harris's 15-move solution for a non-corner start is shown here. Harry Davis found the minimal number of moves required (16) when starting with a missing corner peg.

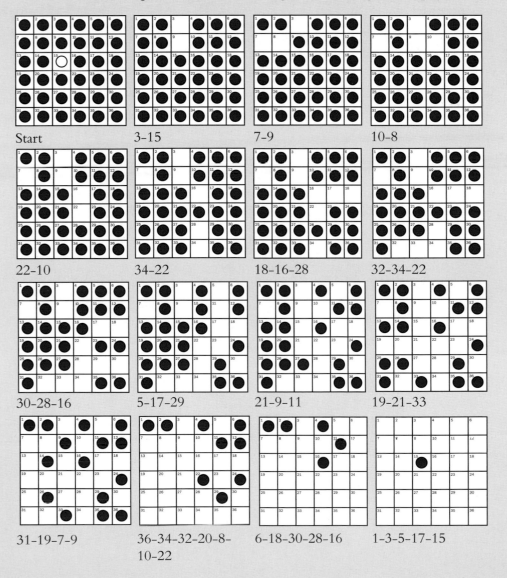

Start   3–15   7–9   10–8

22–10   34–22   18–16–28   32–34–22

30–28–16   5–17–29   21–9–11   19–21–33

31–19–7–9   36–34–32–20–8–10–22   6–18–30–28–16   1–3–5–17–15

▶ GUITAR STRING (page 83)

The pieces of paper at 4 and 6 will jump off when the string starts vibrating.

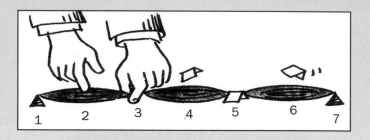

▶ HEXAGONAL NON-MATCHING PUZZLE (page 84)

A gemlike shape—one of the possible solutions.

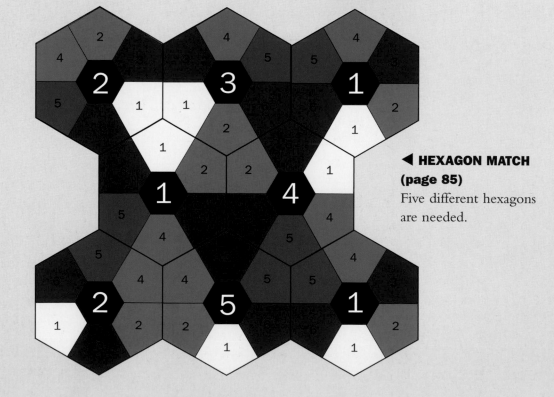

◀ HEXAGON MATCH (page 85)

Five different hexagons are needed.

▶ **QUEENS' ATTACK 1
(page 86)**

Five queens are
sufficient, as shown at
right.

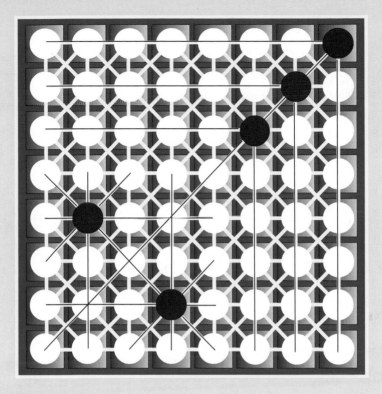

▶ **QUEENS' ATTACK
2 (page 87)**

Five queens are
sufficient, as shown at
right.

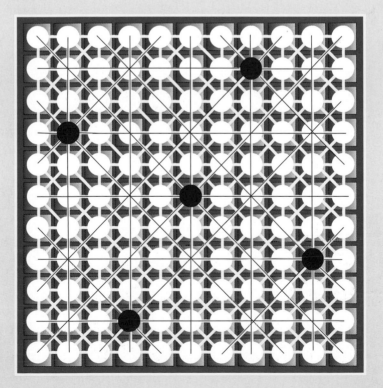

▼ WEIGHING EIGHT COINS (page 88)

The eight coins are divided into two groups of three and a pair.

No matter which group the false coin is in, two weighings are sufficient to find it, as shown below.

Outcome one: First weighing results in equilibrium. One of the two remaining coins must be the false coin.

The second weighing reveals the false coin —whichever is lighter.

Outcome two: The first weighing is unequal. The false coin must be among the three on the right.

When weighing the three coins from the right, if the scales are unequal, the lighter coin is the false coin.

If the scales are in equilibrium on the second weighing, the false coin is the one not yet weighed.

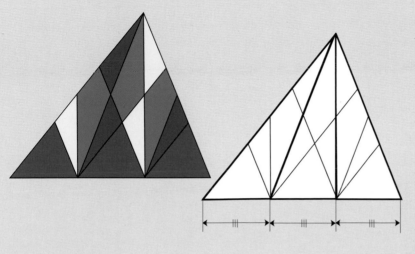

◄ TRIANGLES IN A TRIANGLE (page 89)
You can construct a similar set of pieces for any triangle. Divide the base of a triangle into three equal segments, marking the trisecting pounts with dots. Then draw four lines from both dots: two lines parallel to the other sides of the triangle, one line to the top vertex of the triangle, and one line parallel to the line that extends from the other dot to the top vertex. (All lines should stay within the triangle, stopping when they reach an edge.) Cut along the resulting borders.

▼ MORE SQUARE ROUTES (page 90)

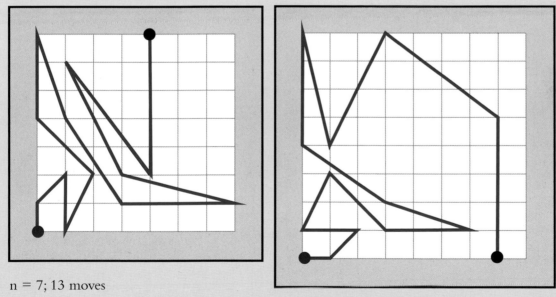

n = 7; 13 moves

n = 8; 13 moves

▼ **CONSECUTIVE RECTANGLES (page 91)**
The total area of the rectangles is 870 square units, equivalent to a
29-by-30 rectangle. The best packing I could obtain is shown below.
   All but the 1-by-3 rectangle were packed in the gameboard.
   Can you do better?

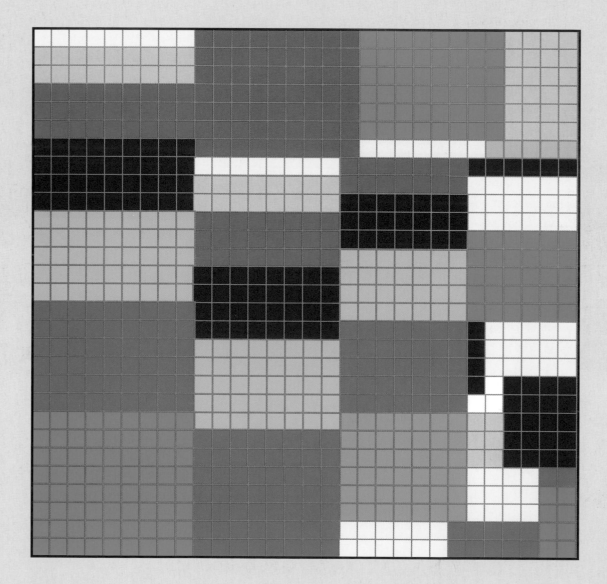